BORLEY POSTSCRIPT

The pictures on the front cover show Borley Rectory as it was
before the fire; Borley Rectory on fire; Borley Church in the 1920s
(a postcard sent to Ethel Bull and now in the possession of the
author); and an oil painting of the Rectory cottage in 1948
(in the possession of the author).

For
my wife Joyce
who made it all possible

BORLEY POSTSCRIPT

by

Peter Underwood

WHITE HOUSE PUBLICATIONS

First published in Great Britain 2001
by
WHITE HOUSE PUBLICATIONS
Box 65 Haslemere Surrey GU27 1XT

ISBN 0-9537721-1-X

Produced by
The Short Run Book Company Limited
St Stephen's House
Arthur Road
Windsor
Berkshire SL4 1RY

CONTENTS

PHOTOGRAPHIC ILLUSTRATIONS

ACKNOWLEDGEMENTS

The author wishes to express his very real gratitude and appreciation to everyone who has co-operated with him on this project and especially, in alphabetical order: Ronald Blythe, Mrs S.M. Brotherwood, Tony Broughall, P.I. Thomas Brown, Katie Burgess, Rev. John C. Dening, Harry Dewhurst, Wesley Downes, Veronica Elelman, Stewart P. Evans, Alan Gregson, Paull Harrap, Rose Holt, Louis Mayerling, Lucie Meeker, Marion Neville, Vincent O'Neil, John L. Randall, 'Ray' (Raymond G. Sandford), Alan Roper, Alan Wesencraft, Eric White, the BBC, Daily Mirror, Dorling Kindersley, East Anglian Magazine, Ghost Club Society, Harry Price Library, University of London, Pen Press Publishers, Society of Authors, Society for Psychical Research and Suffolk Free Press. During the course of this book a little repetition is inevitable, I'm afraid, and some inconsistency.

Every effort has been made to contact all concerned but in a few instances it has not been possible to obtain direct permission and if any copyright has been inadvertently infringed the author and publisher apologise in advance and undertake to make appropriate acknowledgement in future editions.

INTRODUCTION

During the course of moving after nearly thirty years at Bentley in Hampshire I came across a quantity of material and illustrations pertaining to the famous Borley Rectory haunting that had never been published in book form and the seed of the idea for this small volume was planted. Subsequently later material came to my notice and I began to visualize the book in its present form.

A lot of water has flowed under bridges since I first became interested in the subject of Borley Rectory – nearly sixty years in fact – and I count myself very fortunate in having met so many of the leading characters in this dramatic case of apparent haunting and to have been instrumental in organizing a number of lectures and events pertaining to the case including illustrated talks at the London Savage Club (where Harry Price was once a member) and various historic buildings and universities; memorable meals at The Bull, Long Melford, followed by guided tours of Borley; contributions to books, magazines and scientific journals; and the friendship of people like the Bulls, the Foysters, the Whitehouses, the Glanvilles, the Hennings, the Turners, Constance Price, Robert Aickman and many, many more.

All things considered I decided the time had come to release some of this unpublished material and to present for Borley enthusiasts a kind of postscript to all that has been published on Borley up to the present time.

Peter Underwood
Savage Club
1, Whitehall Place
London SW1A 2HD

PART 1

A Pictorial History of the Borley Haunting
(script)

NORTH BEDFORDSHIRE DISTRICT LIBRARIES & EASTERN ARTS ASSOCIATION

PETER UNDERWOOD

The Most Haunted House In England

A pictorial history of Borley Rectory and its ghosts.

BEDFORD CENTRAL LIBRARY

A Pictorial History of the Borley Haunting

[This is the script of a 100-slide lecture which I presented on invitation to, among others, members of The Royal Photographic Society, The Ghost Club Society, The Society for Psychical Research and at such venues as Cambridge, Bedford, Birmingham, Sheffield and at Essex Hall off the Strand beside the historic Watergate, once part of the garden of Essex House, the palatial residence of Robert Devereux, Queen Elizabeth I's favourite and also used by Bonnie Prince Charlie in 1750. This lecture was attended by such people as Dr Eric J. Dingwall, Mrs K.M. Goldney, Dr Letitia Fairfield, Robert J. Hastings, Flight-Lieut R. Carter Jonas, Ellic Howe and Robert Aickman. The latter visited Borley as one of Harry Price's observers and he regarded this lecture as 'the finest appraisal of the Borley haunting' that he had ever heard. Presented without precise details of the placement of the slides it presents a useful introduction to the haunting of Borley Rectory, 'the most haunted house in England'.]

Good evening. For almost as long as I can remember for me the most convincing of all reports of ghosts and haunted houses, mainly because of the length of time that the haunting has apparently persisted and in view of the varied, reliable and considerable number of witnesses, has been the haunting of Borley Rectory on the borders of Essex and Suffolk, long known as 'the most haunted house in England'. Here, if we are to believe reports that go back over a hundred years and continue to this very day – there is or has been a ghost nun, a ghost man, a phantom coach-and-horses, inexplicable footsteps, voices, touchings, smells, fires, movement of objects, written messages, poltergeist phenomena and mysteries galore.

For those unfamiliar with the story Borley Rectory was built in 1863 (on the site of an earlier building, the Herringham rectory) by the Rev. H.D.E. Bull who died in the Blue Room in 1892 and was succeeded by his son the Rev. 'Harry' Bull who died in the same room in 1929. The Bulls, father and son, were therefore incumbents at Borley continuously for sixty-five years. Harry Bull was succeeded by the Rev. G. Eric Smith, an Anglo-Indian who lasted eighteen months and was succeeded in 1930 by the Rev. Lionel Foyster and his wife Marianne and they remained for five years. By this time the ecclesiastical authorities had decided that the property was not a suitable home for the incumbent; the living was combined with neighbouring Liston and the incumbent resided at Liston Rectory. Harry Price, the noted psychic investigator of the day, rented the haunted rectory for a year in 1937; in 1938 the property was sold to Captain W.H. Gregson and the house was gutted by fire in 1939. Various owners of the site sold the bricks and parts of the old rectory land but still the site was reportedly haunted. After the destruction of the rectory the ghosts appeared to transfer their activities to the cottage that had belonged to the Rectory and across the road to the little church of Borley, dedication unknown.

This remarkable case of haunting – and it has to be accepted that everyone who lived there, four successive rectors, their wives and families, all asserted that they heard, saw and felt things they were unable to explain; this unique case has been the subject of five major books, a dozen broadcasts and TV programmes, hundreds of articles all over the world and considerable argument and discussion – and let me say at once that I do not intend to get bogged down this evening in the various arguments about the case and the people involved but to present the generally accepted story of the Borley hauntings.

I first went to Borley in 1947 and spent a night in the grounds accompanied by P.I. Thomas Brown, a Life Member of The Ghost Club Society, and I was there last year. Between these dates I have been to Borley dozens of times, talked to all the local people and personally interviewed practically everyone who has had anything to do with the case.

But now I ask you to come with me out into the broad flat lands of Suffolk and if you take the road from Sudbury towards Long Melford, about a mile before that town you will find an easily-missed turning on your left-hand side. This is Rodbridge Corner and if you take this turning, cross a disused railway line, turn a corner past a couple of cottages and the old village school, you will see a hill ahead of you. And if you climb this hill, Hall Lane, with the open fields on each side, a wild place at most seasons of the year, you will soon catch a glimpse of the tower of Borley Church among the trees on your right. And when you reach the top of the hill and turn your back on the church, you will see a patch of land to the left of the cottage facing you, now altered and built upon, where for years grass and brambles looked like reclaiming the place where once stood Borley Rectory, that house of mystery long known as 'the most haunted house in England'.

But to go back to 1863 when the Rev. H.D.E. Bull built Borley Rectory . . . he had fourteen children and as his family increased, so he added a wing to the house until it became a rambling, rabbit-warren of a place built round an open courtyard but it looks peaceful enough here and indeed it seems to have been a much-loved and well-preserved family home while the Bulls lived there. A picture of old Mrs Bull and five of her daughters, probably taken about 1900 sets the scene for it is from this period that one of the most interesting stories of Borley's ghost nun is told. Three of the Bull sisters, returning from a garden party on a summer evening (28 July 1900) saw, as they turned into the Rectory drive gate, what appeared to be a nun walking along a path in the garden, towards the house; a path that became known as the Nun's Walk. There seemed something unreal about the dark, stooping figure with bowed head, seemingly telling her beads, and while two of the sisters stopped and watched the third sister ran into the house and fetched an older sister, probably Dodie, who came out of the house, saw the figure herself and thinking it was a real Sister of Mercy on some errand or possibly confused and lost, approached the figure but when she was quite close the figure appeared to turn for a moment towards the Rectory – and then it suddenly and completely vanished! Here, if we accept human testimony, we have four independent witnesses to a ghostly figure that is seen from four different viewpoints and I may say here that two of the witnesses who shared that experience related their story to me. Incidentally they told the same story without embellishment or alteration for over fifty years with the result that critics of the case say the sisters had told their stories so often that it was repeated parrot-fashion and had no value as evidence but had they altered the story in the slightest they would have been condemned as telling the story differently each time it was related so they could

12

not be treated seriously as witnesses – so the poor Bull sisters could not be right! On my behalf medical and legal practitioners have considered this matter and agree that it is generally considered that the account one gives of an experience as soon as possible after the experience is likely to be far more accurate than an account given years later. It has to be said that the Bull sisters told a consistent and identical story of the experience from immediately after the event and for the following fifty years.

There are photographs in existence showing old Mrs Bull at the Rectory together with seven of the Bull sisters and it must have been a happy Victorian household in those days. Incidentally those who suggest that the story of the nun haunting Borley Rectory dates back to the reported sighting of the nun in 1900 overlook the fact the old Mrs Bull and her husband knew all about the date the nun was reputed to appear long before 1900 (H.D.E. Bull died in 1892) for a cousin of the Bulls told me that he well remembered staying at the Rectory when one morning at breakfast old Mrs Bull remarked that she thought she had seen the ghost nun in the garden the previous evening and the old rector, the Rev. H.D.E. Bull, had replied that he would not be at all surprised if she had for the previous day had been July 28th, the 'nun's day'.

In the 1920s the shrubbery had grown around Borley Rectory and a pleasant photograph shows Harry Bull with his wife Ivy and her daughter Constance on the tennis court. Harry Bull made no secret of his interest in psychic experiences and he told dozens of people about seeing the ghost nun and hearing a phantom coach-and-horses. Once he said he saw a legless man in the garden and at the same time his dog looked in the direction of the phantom or whatever it was and growled and cowered in fright. The legless man disappeared as he watched.

During the time of the Bulls there are many photographs showing various members of the family outside the south-east verandah at Borley Rectory. They always loved the place but locally it was regarded as haunted. I have talked with a friend of the Bull girls from those days and she told me that she often went to tea with the Bull sisters but people were rarely invited during the evening 'because strange things happened at Borley Rectory at night . . .' All sorts of stories were told about the Rectory. One persistent tale told of a servant being seduced by old Mr Bull and of the resulting child being put to death in the kitchen. The window of the Blue Room is clearly shown in some photographs; this is the room where both H.D.E. Bull and Harry Bull died and where many unexplained happenings were reported.

By now the stories had spread far and wide and a picture appeared in a Canadian newspaper of Borley Rectory with a ghostly nun and coach with headless coachman drawn onto the photograph. It originated from Ernest Ambrose who was organist at Borley Church for sixteen years before the first world war. He had provided a photograph of Borley Rectory to a Canadian journalist who had gone back to Canada, had the photograph 'doctored' and then published it. A legend long associated with Borley says that a monastery once occupied the site of the Rectory and that a lay brother fell in love with a novice from a nearby nunnery; they arranged to elope and succeeded in getting away in a coach but they were soon missed, their superiors gave chase, the coach was overtaken and the couple brought back to face judgement: the lay brother being hanged and the novice bricked-up alive. As far as can be ascertained no monastery ever existed at Borley, nor was there a nunnery nearby so perhaps the story was concocted principally to account for the ghost nun and phantom coach-and-horses which certainly seem to have been heard and seen on many occasions by different people.

The Rectory was build around a courtyard and H.D.E. Bull affixed a great bell high up in the courtyard so that it could be heard throughout the house and it is reputed to have rung many times without human agency. After the fire the bell was given to Harry Price and it hung at his home at Pulborough for thirty years. After his death and when his widow Constance left the house the Harry Price Estate and the University of London presented it to me and it now hangs at my home, one of the very few relics that exist of haunted Borley Rectory – but I am still waiting for it to ring without human agency!

The drawing room at Borley Rectory in the days of the Bulls was a typical cluttered Victorian room. The pastel sketch of Borley Church shows the church path in a different position to the present one. The dining room at Borley Rectory at the same period shows the monk fireplace that is said to have been exhibited at the Great Exhibition at the Crystal Palace in Hyde Park London in 1851 while the portrait in oils of the Rev. H.D.E. Bull followed the surviving members of the family into the 1950s when I saw it at Chilton Lodge, Sudbury, Suffolk where the family ended up.

A framed photograph that hung for years in Borley Church, beside the steps leading up the tower, showed the Rev. Harry Bull and the church choir in 1911. One of the younger members told me that on one occasion he wanted to have a word with the rector and he went to the Rectory one evening but as he approached the front door he saw a dark robed figure about to enter the porch so seeing that the rector had a visitor, the choir boy decided to see the rector another time. When he did so next day he said he had called at the Rectory the previous evening but seeing he had a visitor he had gone away. Harry Bull said he had no visitor that evening but when the boy said he had seen a dark robed figure, the rector quickly interjected . . .'oh, that would be the 'nun', she was very active last night . . .'

The Rev. Harry Bull has been described to me as a 'puckish, lovable man'. It was said he would hail a spectre as easily and unperturbed as anyone else would hail a friend but Dr Prewer, who was at Oxford with Harry Bull, described him to me as 'one of the most normal men you could meet'. He became a typical squire-parson who potted rabbits on the lawn and used to boast of breaking his own record at taking matins. He used to give Latin lessons to boys at Borley Rectory and Jack Harley of Cavendish told me that on one occasion he was at the rectory when a terrific thunder storm broke out and the rector invited the boy to spend the night at the rectory. They talked of life and death and the after-life and Harry Bull commented that what had always struck him was the mundane and ordinary things that the spirits always seemed to do when they returned, make tapping noises, sound footsteps, and so on, 'If I can return after my death,' said Harry Bull. 'I shall do something really different, something unusual so that you know it is me – like throwing mothballs about; yes, if mothballs are thrown after I die, you'll know it's me!' In fact, many years later, long after the death of Harry Bull, some investigators entering the empty house were greeted by a shower of moth-balls!

Ethel Bull took part in several television and radio programmes. She was one of the last surviving sisters and she not only saw the ghost nun on that memorable 28th July 1900 but again a few

15

months later together with the rectory's cook who also saw the figure; Ethel also saw an indistinct human shape in her bedroom and the ghostly figure of a man in a tall hat inside the Rectory; she heard the great bell peal without explanation, heard inexplicable footsteps many times and twice awakened to find a human form in her bedroom, a form that suddenly and mysteriously vanished.

On one of my visits to Chilton Lodge Ethel Bull and her brother Alfred posed for a photograph with me outside their delightful home. They were charming people and lived very much in the present but they had no doubts whatever that Borley Rectory was haunted.

The Coopers were also interviewed for television. They were servants of the Bulls for many years and occupied the cottage that escaped the fire. One bright moonlit night Cooper awoke to hear the sound of grinding wheels and when he looked out of the window he saw a coach-and-horses dashing out of the Rectory grounds. It appeared to drive across Hall Lane, into the field beside the church and disappear alongside the church. Interestingly enough we discovered that many years ago a road had indeed run beside the church.

At the main drive entrance to Borley Rectory the ghost nun has been reportedly seen on many occasions. This was where the three Bull sisters were when they first saw the nun on 28th July 1900 and in 1929, when the Rectory was empty and deserted, a journeyman carpenter named Fred Cartwright, on his way through Borley early one morning saw a 'sister of mercy' standing by the gate, with a pale face and looking as though she had been crying. He saw her again the following morning and a few days later he saw her yet again and this time as soon as he had passed, he thought he ought to ask whether he could be of any help but when he turned the place where he had seen the distinct figure was completely deserted. Years later, early in 1947, when the property was again vacant and deserted, Dr Peter Hilton-Rowe, a retired Bank of England official, was travelling up the road with a friend when he saw the figure of a nun: by this time of course the Rectory had long completely disappeared and Dr Hilton-Rowe was quickly out of the car but no such figure was anywhere in sight. His companion was looking at Peter Hilton-Rowe as he was talking and so was turned away from the Rectory site and saw nothing. Other visitors have reported strange incidents near the drive gate.

Anglo-Indian Guy Eric Smith took the living of Borley in 1928. He had recently returned to England from India where his English wife had not enjoyed the best of health. They knew nothing of the reputed haunting but very soon curious happenings began to worry them: lights unaccountably appeared in unoccupied rooms and as unaccountably disappeared on investigation, in various rooms; dark forms were encountered inside the rambling Rectory; Mrs Smith saw a coach-and horses in the drive that suddenly was no longer there; Smith heard voices, maids told of seeing the figure of a nun in the garden that disappeared and soon the rector, not knowing what to do, wrote to his paper, the "Daily Mirror". They got in touch with Harry Price who went down to Borley with a reporter. Watching in the garden they thought they glimpsed a dark form on the Nun's Walk; a stone crashed through the glass verandah roof and a candlestick hurtled itself down the stairs, one of a pair they had seen upstairs – and no one was upstairs at the time.

Harry Price was fascinated and he continued, on and off, to investigate the haunted Rectory for the rest of his life. He wrote two full-length books on the case and the former in particular, 'The Most Haunted House in England' reached a wide public. One of those who read it was Canon W.J. Phythian-Adams, the Canon of Carlisle. He wrote to Price and suggested a theory that could have accounted for many of the mysterious happenings; a theory that involved a French nun being murdered at Borley and he told Price that he should dig to substantiate or disprove his theory.

When Price did arrange some excavation of the cellars fragmentary human remains were found in one of the wells; human remains that were eventually buried in Liston churchyard. Before being buried Price had them examined by a dental surgeon who reported that they showed a deep-seated abscess that would have given the owner considerable pain – and the remains were most probably those of a young woman. Practically everyone who saw the ghost nun said she had a sad face or looked as though she had been crying. Incidentally I tried for some years to get the fragmentary human remains disinterred so that I could get them examined and dated – this sort of thing having made great strides in sixty years but partitions to the relevant Member of Parliament, the Bishop of the Diocese, the Archdeacon of Colchester, the Central Synod of the Church of England, even the Home Office, were all to no avail.

But to return to the chronological history of the Borley hauntings. The Smiths put up with the haunting of Borley Rectory for some eighteen months and then left. Perhaps it is understandable for Mrs Smith was so terrified by the mysterious happenings that she used to shriek with fright. After her husband died Mrs Smith became very disturbed and troubled by what had happened, even blaming the disturbances for causing the death of her husband. She ended her days at Sheringham, her memories of Borley confused and unreliable but contemporary evidence exists to show that she and her husband did in fact experience a wealth of unexplained happenings; in fact she wrote a manuscript based on the disturbances entitled "Murder at the Parsonage".

Harry Bull, as we have seen, was fascinated by the ghosts of Borley and he is credited with building a summer house in the garden, facing the Nun's Walk, for the express purpose of watching for the ghost nun. Certainly he spent many hours in the summer house, 'communing with the spirits' and looking for the nun – and seeing her many times, it seems. In 1911 Harry Bull, much against the wishes of his family, married a widowed Roman Catholic with a daughter and soon they moved into Borley Rectory and his sisters moved out.

The Bull sisters moved across the road to Borley Place, a fine sixteenth century house that practically adjoins the church. (The window overlooking the churchyard is false.) H.D.E. Bull had lived at Borley Place while his Rectory was being built. It is not difficult to imagine the disunity that must have existed at Borley Rectory at this time between a Church of England rector and his Roman Catholic wife and her Catholic daughter and by all accounts it seems that Harry Bull and his wife lived in disharmony for many years before he died in the Blue Room – and there were whispers that his wife had helped him on his way. The daughter Constance escaped by marrying when she was eighteen a man much older than herself, Colonel Boothby. She then moved to South Africa where she died in 1970.

There have always been stories of tunnels at Borley, especially between Borley Place and the Rectory, tunnels that have often played a part in the nun and monk story and in unsubstantiated tales of murder and a number of experiments have taken place in an effort to establish the existence of any tunnel. From my own experiments in 1948 I had no doubt that some sort of tunnel existed under the road, evident from a hollow sound in parts.

Harry Price, who came on the scene in 1929, was a most respected physical researcher. He had investigated scores of haunted houses and exposed many mediums although he was quick to endorse any medium he thought genuine. With hauntings too he usually found a mundane explanation but occasionally here too he was not afraid to say that he thought he was faced with genuine paranormal activity. Borley was a challenge and a puzzle to him; at first he thought he had found the answer in fraudulence and deception but later, largely due to the work of his investigators, he came to accept that Borley presented a real problem for the sceptics. Those who have criticized his methods and work at Borley should remember that he was breaking new ground and subjecting a haunted house to scientific exploration for the very first time while those who accuse him of deliberate trickery should remember that for years, right up to his death, he was a devout churchgoer and sidesman at Pulborough Church where he was married, where he is buried and where the rector told he was a man of complete integrity. He was photographed, unusually for him, actually taking part in an investigation, waiting in Harry Bull's summer house for the nun; his camera at the ready.

Some years after Price died in 1948 I went to see his widow, Constance Price, at their home in Pulborough. She had never had any interest in his psychical work but she could not understand the attacks that were levelled at him. 'These people were our friends,' she told me. 'They know it is not true – why do they say these things?' She was referring to Eric Dingwall and Mollie Goldney.

During the course of his lengthy investigation Harry Price and particularly his chief collaborator in the mysteries of Borley, Sidney Glanville, compiled a voluminous manuscript about the case that contained many surmises, suggestions, allegations and libellous statements which they called "The Locked Book of Private Information". I process a complete copy. Many of the people concerned are now dead and much of the material has been published in various books. Long after Price's death Trevor Hall, one of the three authors of the attack on Price, borrowed the "Locked Book" from the Harry Price Library at the University of London and then flatly refused to return it; selling it instead to an American collector for twelve hundred pounds.

The Bull Hotel at Long Melford was the venue for many people visiting Borley, including Price, and many investigators stayed there during their visits to the haunted Rectory, the rectory site, the rectory cottage and the village church. Harry Price and his entourage are still remembered – or were a few years ago – although the place has been much altered and 'improved' over the years. Many years ago the manager and staff thought they had a resident ghost which I investigated – but that is another story.

After the Smiths moved out a cousin of the Bulls, Lionel Foyster, took the living and was the last incumbent to live at Borley Rectory. Foyster was a quiet, cultured, intelligent man but in the five years that he and his much younger wife Marianne lived there, he became completely convinced that paranormal activity took place repeatedly and he produced a manuscript "Fifteen Months in a Haunted House" (of which I possess a copy) which is a fascinating day-by-day record of just a portion of his sojourn in the haunted Rectory. He circulated to family members almost daily accounts of the many curious happenings that he and his wife experienced. He became crippled with arthritis and eventually had to relinquish the living. He had no children himself but he and Marianne brought with them to the Rectory a girl they had adopted, Adelaide, and there were other young children they looked after from time to time.

Marianne Foyster, wife of the Rev. Lionel Algernon Foyster B.A. (known to his friends as 'Lion'), was a bright, vivacious, bouncy type of individual and although she tried to help her husband in the lonely little village, she came to hate the quiet and solitude of Borley. It must have been very difficult for her and both before and after Borley her life was a chequered one. She had married at fifteen a man named Greenwood. There is no record of any divorce but she married Foyster in 1922, describing herself as a spinster. It seems that Foyster had christened her as a young girl. Later, after they left Borley and Foyster was totally bedridden she passed him off as her father and 'married' a commercial traveller named Fisher. After Fisher's death and four months after Foyster died, she 'married' a man named O'Neil and went to America. I was in contact with Marianne for years in America where she lived a quiet life, helping to run an old peoples' home when she was well over eighty! She was born in 1899 in a cottage at Romiley in Cheshire and has been photographed in jocular mood in various poses.

At one period, while living at Borley, Marianne ran a flower shop in London with a man named d'Arles, only returning to Borley at weekends. d'Arles eventually died in Australia.

During one of his visits to Borley Harry Price, Marianne, Lionel Foyster and Mollie Goldney – once a close associate of Harry Price – were photographed together. She became an active member of the Society for Psychical Research (an organization that never really found favour with Harry Price). One of the children at Borley rectory in the 1930s, Adelaide, was put into a home when Marianne went to America and was later traced and re-united with her family by a Ghost Club Society investigator.

During the Foyster occupancy many people asserted that they experienced inexplicable phenomena at Borley Rectory. Guy L'Estrange, a Justice of the Peace, former headmaster of Colchester Grammar School and a very responsible person who maintained that he had seen bottles materialize in front of his eyes was treated contemptuously by the S.P.R. in their Report on Borley and they had to publish an apology.

Many messages appeared on the walls and on scraps of paper at Borley Rectory during the Foyster period. Most had a distinct Catholic flavour, asking for light, mass and prayers; and while a graphologist thought they were all in the same handwriting except one, the unusual height and size of the messages have yet to be explained. Most of them appeared to be addressed to Marianne and once she wrote under the 'message' 'I cannot understand, tell me more', whereupon another message was found underneath but no clearer than the first so Marianne wrote 'I still cannot understand, please tell me more' but nothing more appeared. It was generally agreed that the messages were written by Marianne, perhaps in a state of disassociation; but words and squiggles appeared on the walls long after the Foysters left the Rectory and while it was empty of all human beings; such witnesses include Professor C.E.M. Joad and John Snagg from the BBC who both insisted to me that marks appeared in their presence which could not be explained in terms of normality.

The Rev A.C. Henning became Rector of Borley with Liston and in the main lived at Liston Rectory. Before Borley Rectory was sold Harry Price rented the place for a year and arranged a rota of investigators who conduced scientific exploration and examination of the place, often staying overnight, and still an astonishing array of unexplained happenings took place. At the end of the year the property was sold for £500 and Captain Gregson took up residence with his two sons in 1938.

In February 1939 Borley Rectory, which Gregson had insured for £10,000, was gutted by fire. It is said that the fire was burning for the best part of an hour before the fire brigade arrived; at all events the insurance company were unhappy and refused to pay out. Eventually the matter was settled out of court with a payment of £750. In the short time that he was at Borley Rectory Captain Gregson and his family claimed to experience a number of incidents for which they could find no rational explanation and in fact Captain Gregson appeared on the BBC radio "In Town Tonight" programme talking about his adventures at 'the most haunted house in England'. Even during the fire there were reported incidents that could not be explained such as human figures being seen in the empty window gaps where there was no longer any flooring. A fireman and a policeman were among witnesses for this occurrence and also seeing human figures walking out of the blazing building, 'human' figures that disappeared.

Oddly one spot of flooring remained almost intact. This was the area of the 'cold spot', a place where it was scientifically proved to be colder than the surrounding area, for no apparent reason. This was also the place where the Rev. Eric Smith, passing along the passage one evening, suddenly heard a voice say something that sounded like 'Don't, Carlos, don't . . .' No explanation was ever found for this voice. However there are grounds for believing that Harry Bull was known to his intimates as 'Carlos' and this is something that would certainly not have been known to Smith.

Soon after the fire when visitors and sightseers prowled round the ruins and garden there were reports of strange noises and occasionally strange forms that disappeared in puzzling circumstances and footfalls were heard to sound on floorboards that were no longer there.

In 1944 Harry Price visited the ruins with an American photographer for the purpose of taking some photographs. During the course of the photographic session they took a photograph which seemed to show a brick 'poised in mid-air' as Price put it. Although the ruins were being demolished at the time, Price stated there were no workmen 'on that side of the site'. A statement that would mean little if there were workmen on the other side and they were throwing bricks over and indeed in the published photograph the head of a workman is just visible on the extreme left. However Price said the brick shot up into the air but this is one phenomenon at Borley that I do not think was paranormal. In fact the photographer himself told me that at the time they all laughed at the incident and did not take it at all seriously.

During the second world war Borley was photographed from the air and the Rectory site, the rectory cottage and the church are all plainly visible. Also the close proximity of the farm is apparent which might suggest the possibility of rats producing some of the 'mysterious' sounds yet no one ever reported the possibility of rats or mice and I have spoken to many of Price's investigators and I have examined minutely dozens of photographs of the interior of the Rectory and have never found any of the characteristic holes and scratches caused by such rodents.

After the second world war efforts were made to locate the tunnels that have been reported from time to time and a plan of the excavated ruins showed the site of the two wells which were fully explored without revealing any more bones. The plan also shows the undoubted remains of foundations of a former building or buildings. I discovered a Tithe Map of 1841 showing the former rectory on the site of haunted Borley Rectory but we have little information concerning the history of that building or buildings.

In 1957 workmen digging a trench between the church and the Rectory site cut through brickwork and exposed the long-lost tunnel. It ran underneath the road and could have accounted for some of the hollow sounds reported from the direction of the roadway over the years. The tunnel in parts was in almost perfect condition, the bricks red two-inch Tudor type and in all probability it was a conduit of some kind but it was certainly large enough to have been used as a bolt hole. The workmen found it blocked by rubble at both ends.

When I first saw the Rectory site in 1947 the cottage and grounds had just been purchased by James Turner, the poet and novelist, and he and his wife Catherine experienced many apparently inexplicable incidents. Once a phantom cat invaded the cottage; on several occasions they heard loud crashing noises that had no explanation and once Cathy, sitting in a deck chair on the site of the old Rectory, then a grassy patch, heard heavy and distinct footsteps approaching behind her; she looked round but nothing was visible although the footsteps still sounded as though they were approaching. She sat still and the distinct footfalls came quite close to her, walked all round her and then went away; but the puzzling thing is that they sounded as though they were walking on echoing floorboards as though the Rectory was still there but of course the Rectory had long disappeared and there was only grass all round her.

James Turner was a gardener and he outlined the site of the haunted Rectory with a low brick wall and preserved the Nun's Walk. Once when he was working on the overgrown bushes and brambles, bringing to light the old paths that had been buried for so long, he heard the sound of happy, laughing voices ahead of him. He called to Cathy and she too heard the voices. James thought he would reach the voices and he suddenly burst through the dense bushes hoping to catch up with them but, as he put it, 'the voices, happy and laughing, fled before me . . .' After some four years the Turners left Borley, they said it was the constant flood of unexpected visitors who wanted to see where once stood the haunted Rectory rather than the ghosts that caused them to leave. They went to Belchamp Walter, then Grundisburgh and finally Cornwall where they both died years later. I remained friends with the Turners for more than forty years and often think kindly of them.

One day I heard from the Turners and there was excitement for a stone face was uncovered in an old wall. Ronald Blythe, later a prominent writer on English rural life, was staying with the Turners at the time. Ronnie was kind enough to draw the face and send it to me. Already it was being suggested that perhaps the positioning of the face in the wall marked the place where something was buried . . . but when next I saw Ethel Bull I asked her about the face and showed her the drawing. She couldn't remember it clearly but thought it was probably something that had been found in the garden, or possibly in the churchyard, and Harry Bull had built it into the wall that he was working on. 'That's the sort of thing Harry did . . .' she said. Another mystery solved – well, probably solved!

During one of the radio broadcasts that they recorded at Borley Tom Gooch was interviewed. He had worked for James Turner for a while and he and his wife had then bought a slice of the old Rectory ground and had built themselves a bungalow. Mrs Gooch encountered several puzzling incidents including the finding of a rosary, seeing a figure in the garden and witnessing movement of objects in the church. Tom Gooch also testified to movement of objects and spoke of strange noises at night.

Borley Church, where many of the actors in the Borley drama lie buried and a place known to all of them has undoubtedly been the scene of inexplicable happenings from ghostly figures, phantom music and footsteps to interference with instruments (unexplained jamming, uncontrolled switching on and off, mysterious recording, etc). Once a visiting clergyman, previously a sceptic of the ghosts of Borley, told me that as he waited to officiate at the funeral of a friend, he heard footsteps approaching the porch and, thinking the local rector had arrived to meet him, he left the enclosed porch. He then saw the figure of a nun in the churchyard, she disappeared behind a bush which the Rev. Kipling immediately approached when she did not reappear; there was nobody behind the bush and nothing that could have accounted for what he saw. The Rev. Stanley Kipling is now much less sceptical of Borley and its mysteries. Actually the church porch has been the centre of a number of incidents. Many people sheltering there have heard footsteps, voices, music and have never found any rational explanation. On one occasion James Turner was sitting in the church porch, idly thinking that he was completely happy when he heard footsteps approaching along the church path; as he decided whether to get up or stay where he was he noticed that the footsteps walked with a limp and a swishing sound accompanied the footfalls; almost like someone wearing a long dress. There was nothing to be seen when James eventually left the porch and the sounds ceased immediately. It was a night of the full moon and there was not a thing in sight.

The Bacons brought the place from the Turners and after the Bacons the place was bought by a man named Martin who never lived there but he made considerable alterations and improvements including partial solar heating and soon the place was on the market again, this time for £87,000.

Many people who visited Borley have found their photographic equipment malfunction, although everything was worked perfectly before coming to Borley and works perfectly after leaving Borley: could it be that there is something in that enchanted area that we do not yet understand? Others find they have caught something quite unexpected on the resulting prints and I have seen literally hundreds of photographs taken at Borley where it is possible to see a figure or figures that were not present to the photographer. Personally I feel sure such pictures are unusually the result of an unusual combination of light and shade or some equally mundane explanation but very, very occasionally I am not so sure . . .

Among the parties I have taken to Borley have been members of The Ghost Club Society and they have included Dr Peter Hilton-Rowe, Mrs Cecil Baines, a Roman Catholic who researched the idea of a French nun being murdered at Borley, Raymond Armes who took lots of photographs at Borley some of which included puzzling additions, Brig. C.A.L. Brownlow, James Wentworth Day who saw a phantom cat at Borley, Mr and Mrs Guy L'Estrange and Granville Squiers the author of "Secret Hiding Places".

Among the television programmes that included shots of Borley "The Ghost Hunters" showed me visiting the church and talking on the roadway with my back to the Rectory site, relating the story of the haunting. Hugh Burnett produced this programme as he had produced an earlier one about Borley. He told me that when he began to work on the programme he was very sceptical but later he was less so and ready to accept that some of the experiences related were very difficult to explain in rational terms.

Among other visits to Borley was one where we enjoyed a meal at The Bull, Long Melford, followed by a talk by a local enthusiast (there are not many of them!) and a visit to the site when those present included Ghost Club Society member Alan Roper who went to America and talked with Marianne and traced Adelaide who had lived at Borley Rectory at the time of the Foysters.

At one time dowsing was carried out at Borley over several days when the Rev. Henning disclosed that he felt the lost plate of Borley Church might be buried somewhere on the site. A dowser from Long Melford spent hours looking and working the site but to no avail. Each evening she would leave her dowsing twig in a tree and each morning it would be found a hundred yards away. The cottage was empty and the site vacant at the time. Eventually she became convinced that 'something' was buried beneath an enormous walnut tree but digging to a depth of over nine feet revealed nothing of interest; the night after they filled in the hole there was a tremendous storm and the walnut tree was uprooted and fell exactly where the digging had taken place.

Also at one time a lot of work was done to discover the entrance to the elusive crypt in Borley Church. It was thought the entrance might be beneath the nave and Alfred Henning and his wife and James Turner obtained the necessary permission and dug. All they did was break into a tomb other than discovering a pre-Reformation altar. Years later it was reported that an entrance had been discovered in the churchyard behind some railings but nothing of interest was located.

The Rev. A.C. Henning became deeply interested in the Borley hauntings and from his induction in 1936 to his sudden death in 1955 he never lost his enthusiasm and he experienced a wealth of apparently paranormal activity, together with his wife and two sons, seeing a ghost hand, hearing ghostly music and ghostly footsteps and movement of objects on innumerable occasions. He compiled an interesting booklet "Haunted Borley", which James Turner typed for him on condition that there was no mention of the experiences of the Turners, and it sold well and is now something of a collectors' item. Henning was a friendly man, perhaps a little gullible, but he always tried to be helpful and readily assisted genuine seekers after truth.

During the course of one television film young Terry Bacon, the son of the then occupants of the cottage, was interviewed and he related how he had twice seen the figure of a nun in the old Rectory garden and once it had disappeared through a hedge although the hedge did not move. His grandfather, who also lived at the cottage, said he had seen the figure of a nun in the garden on one occasion, through the window of a chicken house where he was at the time. By the time he was out of the chicken house there was no sign of the 'nun'.

The Waldegraves were an important family and considerable land owners in the area years ago and the impressive Waldegrave tomb dominates Borley Church. It has been suggested that a member of the Waldegrave family was responsible for the murder that may have sparked off the haunting; alternatively it has been implied that the daughter of the family who is unnamed on the tomb might be Arabella, a possible contender for the ghost nun according to some researchers.

Among responsible witnesses for sightings of the nun was a local physician, Dr Abernethy. She was on her way to visit a patient and passing the Rectory site noticed the figure of a stooping nun close to the hedge. At first taking the figure for a real person, she suddenly recalled stories of the ghost nun of Borley and she hastily applied the brakes and backed the car down past the Rectory site but there was no trace of anybody at the spot where she had distinctly seen the figure of a sad-looking nun. She even got out of her car and had a good look all round but the place was deserted.

The interior of Borley Church has been altered over the years and practically nothing remains of the original wall pictures. Interestingly enough scores of visitors have reported hearing footsteps follow them as they have walked up the aisle of the church and especially when those present have had their minds on the original pictures that once graced the church walls. Indeed recordings have been obtained of unexplained footsteps in Borley Church.

The little organ at Borley Church has apparently played by itself on many occasions – this is interesting since it would need a ghostly pumper for the air as well as a ghostly player to produce the music! Strange clicking sounds have been reported from the immediate vicinity of the Waldegrave tomb, 'like earth falling', which perhaps it is. Visiting Borley Church Michael Bentine's father, who was very psychic, suddenly stopped and said he could not go on: there was an invisible presence stopping him. Other visitors have reported hearing the sound of a single sigh. The north door of the church has long been bricked up.

A very fine model of Borley Rectory is interesting since it presents a view of the Rectory that was never possible with the actual Rectory, a high hedge running close between Hall Lane and the front entrance porch, the door used by so many odd people who reported so many odd happenings at this very odd house.

Whatever one's personal conclusions on the wide variety of apparent phenomena witnessed at Borley Rectory and thereabouts it is a sobering thought that if just one of these reportedly paranormal happening could be scientifically established and accepted, it would be necessary for us to face the fact that our physical account of the world is incomplete. Thank you for your very kind attention.

* * * * * *

Borley Rectory c. 1895 with old Mrs H.D.E. Bull on the verandah with her son the Rev. Harry Bull together with seven of the Bull sisters.

Walter Bull who spent most of his life in the Navy. A framed picture that once hung in Borley Rectory now in the possession of the author.

PART 2

"The Haunted Rectory"

1947 broadcast (script)

'THE
**HAUNTED
RECTORY'**

*An impartial investigation by
Peter Eton and Alan Burgess
into the strange events at a
lonely Essex rectory*

TONIGHT AT 9.30

"The Haunted Rectory"

[This is the full script of the BBC 1947 broadcast prepared at the initiation of Harry Price and with his collaboration. Contributors include Harry Price himself, Sidney Glanville, Ethel Bull, Rev. and Mrs Henning, the Coopers, Captain Gregson and James Turner]

"The Haunted Rectory" No. 10 in the True Escape Stories

An impartial investigation by PETER ETON and ALAN BURGESS into the strange "goings on" at a lonely Essex Rectory.

Those taking part include: MR HARRY PRICE, PETER ETON, ALAN BURGESS, MR LESLIE KEMP, REV. HENNING, MRS HENNING, MISS ETHEL BULL, MR COOPER, MRS COOPER, MR SAMUEL SEAL, MR GLANVILLE, CAPT. GREGSON, MR RUSSELL, MR & MRS GOOCH, MR TURNER, MR WALTER BAIRD.

with

Cecile Cheuvreau, Gwen Day Burroughs, Frank Partington, Brian Powley, Charles Maunsell, Duncan McIntrye and Marjorie Westbury.

The programme edited by ALAN BURGESS, based on material contained in HARRY PRICE's two books, 'THE END OF BORLEY RECTORY' and 'THE MOST HAUNTED HOUSE IN ENGLAND' – with additional material supplied by those who took part in the programme and MR ERNEST HARDY, MR SHAW JEFFREY, MR HERBERT MAYES, MRS PEARSON & LADY WHITEHOUSE. PRODUCED BY PETER ETON BBC Home Service 29 June 9.30-10.15 p.m.

RECORDINGS

MONDAY, 16TH JUNE: At Borley, MR. GOOCH, MR. TURNER, MRS. GOOCH, MR. KEMP

TUESDAY, 17TH JUNE: At Borley. MR. COOPER, MRS. COOPER, MISS ETHEL BULL, MR. SAMUEL SEAL. MR. RUSSELL. ALAN BURGESS. PETER ETON.

WEDNESDAY, 18TH JUNE: At Maldon. CAPTAIN GREGSON.

TUESDAY, 24TH JUNE: At B.H. MR. HARRY PRICE. REVEREND HENNING. MRS. HENNING. MR. GLANVILLE. GWEN DAY BURROUGHS. FRANK PARTINGTON. MARJORIE WESTBURY.

THURSDAY, 20TH JUNE: At B.H. MR. HARRY PRICE. PETER ETON.

FRIDAY, 27TH JUNE: SOUND EFFECTS.

* * * * * *

SATURDAY, 28TH JUNE: 2.00 p.m. – 6.00 p.m. Rehearsal with cast recordings and effects. LANGHAM HOTEL.

SUNDAY, 29TH JUNE: 10.00 a.m. – 2.00 p.m. Rehearse. STUDIO 1. STAGE DOOR CANTEEN.

3.30 p.m. – 9.30 p.m. Rehearse. STUDIO 2.

TRANSMISSION: 9.30 p.m. – 10.15 p.m. HOME SERVICE.

"ESCAPE"

NO. 10. 'The Haunted Rectory'

ANNOUNCER: This is the BBC Home Service. We present the tenth programme in the series of escape stories – The Haunted Rectory.

(MUSIC: INTRODUCTORY BARS – TO BACKGROUND FOR:

This is the true story of an investigation into the strange 'goings on' at a lonely Essex rectory. It's a ghost story.

PSYCHIC RESEARCHER: My dear sir, nobody knows what it is. Perhaps it's the unhappy ghost of a nun seeking rest – seeking escape from the half world she was left in by some dreadful deed of the past.

(MUSIC UP AND BEHIND)

ANNOUNCER: In the Home Counties there are scores of old houses with ghostly legends of "things that go bump in the night" and eerie white shades that return on the midnight chime. Tonight we present an investigation undertaken by Peter Eton and Alan Burgess of perhaps the most inexplicable case of haunting of them all at – the Haunted Rectory.

(MUSIC UP AND CROSSFADES INTO GHOSTLY WIND)

RECTOR: I heard a voice outside in the darkness. A woman's voice crying pitifully –

WOMAN: Don't Carlos – don't –

RECTOR: There it is again. Listen

WOMAN: Don't Carlos – don't –

GIRL: Elsie, Elsie, I've just seen the nun again. The other side of the garden. She looked at me then – disappeared. I was terrified – terrified –

(WIND UP AND BEHIND)

YOKEL: I tell you I saw the coach. Coming across the field towards me. Not making a sound. Two lights on it and a coachman. And then it disappeared! And all those bangings and knockings?

PSYCHIC RESEARCHER: (*crash of tray of crockery – then knockings*) Poltergeists my dear sir. Knocks – footsteps – things being thrown about – there's no natural, logical explanation for the things they do. We call it paranormal activity.

(*WIND UP AND BEHIND*)

WOMAN: (*bells jangle behind speech*) They're ringing again. All of them. And there's no one near them. They're ringing by themselves.

3RD WOMAN: (*close to hysteria*) I can't stay here I tell you. There's something evil about the place – something dreadful must have happened years ago. I won't stay here. It's haunted – haunted . . .

(*SUDDENLY FURY OF BELLS – HAMMERINGS – CROCKERY AND GLASS BREAKING ARE DROWNED BY WIND RISING TO CLIMAX THEN SLOWLY FADE OUT*)

PETER ETON: Ghosts? Nonsense. All these things you've just heard about – noises, manifestations, apparitions? Impossible. That was how we thought anyway. All right for "Appointment With Fear". But not true. Not the sort of thing that actually happens. And yet – we'd read Mr. Harry Price's two well known books on the alleged hauntings, and there was no doubt that the evidence he presented was extremely impressive. Two hundred reputable witnesses vouched for the most amazing happenings. Could there possibly be something in it? And if so could we find out?

ALAN BURGESS: That was how it started. Could we find out? We were two normal, sceptical young men with no axes to grind. If we interviewed and recorded all the principle witnesses would that solve anything? Supposing we presented the evidence as

35

impartially as we could – the people who believed the story – the people who said it was nonsense. Would that solve the mystery? For no doubt about it, it was a strange story.

NARRATOR: Yes, it's a strange story. Almost a hundred years ago – in 1863 – the Reverend Henry Bull decided to build a new rectory in a remote Essex hamlet. He built it on the site of a much older house – and so they say – on the site of an old monastery. It was a vast, austere, red brick house built in Victorian-Gothic style, and the Reverend Henry Bull raised a large family – twelve children in all. But from the first it seemed that there was something rather odd about the place.

1ST VOICE: A ghostly nun was alleged to wander about the gardens.

2ND VOICE: And even peer through the dining room windows.

3RD VOICE: A spectral coach was seen: driving down the lane.

4TH VOICE: There were knockings and other peculiar noises.

5TH VOICE: And perhaps stranger still was the fact that none of the Bull family seemed to bother about them very much – they just took it all for granted.

NARRATOR: In 1892 The Reverend <u>Henry</u> Bull died and his son the Reverend <u>Harry</u> Bull took over the living. And the strange phenomena still continued. The years passed, and other rectors arrived. The same things happened – even increased. Then in 1936 the ecclesiastical authorities decided the house was redundant and offered it for sale. Harry Price the well known psychic researcher rented it for a year and a rota of investigators under his direction kept it under constant observation. In 1938 a Captain Gregson purchased it, and in 1939 it was almost completely gutted by fire. But even fire did not seem to deter the ghosts.

Today, Well, let's go back on the story and try to get the whole thing in perspective. The present rector of the district is the Reverend Henning – he lives just down the road from the site of the old rectory. Here is his story:–

REVEREND HENNING: I've been rector here for ten years. And in my mind there's no doubt at all that the rectory is a genuine haunt. You see, so many of my friends – people I know – people who, I'm sure, would never tell me lies – have heard and seen things. There are too many reliable witnesses for them all to be mistaken. I found the old house extremely gloomy and depressing. I've never actually seen anything but one or two rather unexplainable things have happened to me. I remember one night in particular, the house was empty at the time. My wife and I and a friend were in the base room.

MRS HENNING: Yes, we were in the base room and not feeling at all ghostly. And then suddenly we heard footsteps coming along the corridor outside. It gave us quite a start because you see all the doors were locked and no one could get in. The footsteps started very faintly and got louder – just as if someone was coming towards us. And as they got closer we distinctly heard the swish of trailing skirts. Oh yes, it scared us for a second. Then my husband said, "Open the door quickly". We jumped up and pulled it open. But the footsteps suddenly stopped and the corridor was empty.

NARRATOR: Eton and Burgess heard that story on a sunny June afternoon. And it shook them a little. A sunny afternoon in June and a respectable sane clerical gentleman telling them without blinking an eyelid that he's sure the place is a genuine haunt. So they went up to see the site of the haunted rectory themselves. Let me tell you about it. Let me try and show you on the radio something of the peculiar atmosphere – the feeling of the place. Music please.

(MUSIC BEGINS SOFTLY IN BACKGROUND)

READER: Follow a long narrow road stretching up between the low green hedges. A narrow inviting road – leading upwards and onwards so straight it might have been a Roman highway. Realise that for centuries this land was Roman. And understand that when their civilisation crumbled the Danes came in from the low coastline and up the marshy rivers.

Yes, old country – old invasion country with a history stretching back beyond man's memory.

Up the narrow road to the hillcrest, and into a circle of tall dark trees. Into an oasis of deep shadow. To the south the meadows slope to a quiet river; the fields are a foot high in green corn; the sunshine fills every field in the sleeping countryside. But inside the green circle of deep shade a quietness, a stillness. A little church with a square tower. A graveyard. Old yew trees. The foundations of the haunted rectory. Yes, it is a little eerie. Even the unwary can sense the atmosphere. You see – so many strange things have happened here.

(MUSIC SLOWLY FADES. AND ENDS)

NARRATOR: Frankly that was a melodramatic trick – purposely overdrawn. But it was done purposely to make you feel the peculiar atmosphere that breeds over the rectory ruins. Now back to Eton and Burgess. Like all good ghost-hunters they decided to pass the night there. They explored the grounds. They poked their noses into the shadows. They waited hopefully among the rectory ruins – then just before midnight –

(FADE AND THEN UP INTO:)

DISC 15 BURGESS AND ETON.

ETON: You stay over there and see if you can hear anything, I'll stay this side.

BURGESS: Quiet, isn't it. I suppose all this rubbish is where the cellar used to be.

ETON: Old wrappings, according to Harry.

BURGESS: We'll never hear a ghost tonight. What's the time?

ETON: Eleven o'clock. They say the ghost walks at midnight, doesn't it?

BURGESS: I think it does, yes.

(*TAPPING BEGINS*)

ETON: Sh-sh. Look, listen. Come over here. Listen!

BURGESS: It's a cricket.

ETON: No, it's not.

BURGESS: It's the wind, then.

ETON: No. Sounds like two bricks tapping, doesn't it.

BURGESS: Amongst all this rubbish here it might be anything. It's probably a rat.

ETON: It's peculiar.

(*TAPPING BEGINS AGAIN*)

BURGESS: There you are – this is incredible. Sounds like morse tapping.

ETON: Speak to me whoever you are.

BURGESS: This is incredible. I would have never believed this.

(*DIE AWAY EFFECTS*)

And we assure you that it is an <u>accurate</u> reconstruction of what actually happened to Peter Eton and myself. Perhaps it was a rat – a cricket? What else could it be? But the more we thought about that noise afterwards the more convinced we were that there was no logical explanation for the cause of it.

NARRATOR: "What else could it be?" A hundred people have echoed that question. And no one knows for certain. Perhaps no one will ever know. You needn't believe it. You can say all these people are telling deliberate lies. You can say that their eyes and their ears deceived them. You can say that the recordings you are going to hear are faked. You can say you don't believe in ghosts. But this is the evidence. Mr. Hardy, for example, who lives in the village. This is his story:-

ERNEST HARDY: As long as I can remember the villagers have said there was something queer going on up at the rectory. But no one knew quite what. Sort of vague rumours. I knew a man called Thompson – he's dead now – who used to go up and play dominoes with Mr. Harry Bull. One evening he went up and saw a nun come out of the back porch and cross over to the church. So he decided the parson had company and went home. The next night the same thing happened, and the night after that. The fourth night he met Parson Bull who said, "Where've you been the last few nights, Harry?" "I saw the nun coming out of the back door and going across to the church," says Thompson. "I didn't like to bother you while you'd got company." And Parson Bull said, "Oh you don't want to bother about her, she's always around."

NARRATOR: Second hand evidence you say? All right. Let's go back and start at the beginning. Who can tell us of that first period before 1900 when the Reverend Henry Bull and his large family lived there? Here, first of all, is Mr. Shaw Jeffrey's story – he was headmaster of Colchester Royal Grammar School:-

MR. JEFFREY: Harry the eldest son of Henry Bull and I were born in the same year 1862. We went to Oxford together and in the long vacations I used to go and stay with him at the rectory. I had lots of small adventures there. Stones falling about; my boots found on top of the wardrobe. I saw the nun several times and often heard the spectral coach go clattering by. In fact I heard the ghostly coach-and-four sweep down the much too narrow lane beside the rectory so often that I could sleep through the noise. Several adult members of the family saw the nun comparatively often, and Harry Bull who spent a good deal of time in the summer house was especially favoured. The smaller children treated the whole thing as a joke. But the biggest adventure in my opinion was the time I lost a big French dictionary which I had been using regularly for some days. Nobody could find it. Then one night I was awakened by a big bump on the floor and there was the dictionary (after I had lit my candle) with it's back a good deal knocked about, sprawling on the floor. And my bedroom door was locked.

NARRATOR: An odd story, isn't it? Now another reputable witness of the same period. Miss Ethel Bull, who was born in the rectory and lived there for over thirty years. She grew up in the atmosphere.

DISC 12:

MISS ETHEL BULL: My father was the rector and we lived there for many years, we were a large family, twelve of us in fact. And we were happy, and nothing happened, we never knew anything about the nun, and the noises in the house – there were a few noises, but they never disturbed us, and we never thought anything of it. And I shared a bedroom with one of my sisters and every night, I suppose it would be somewhere between nine and ten, there used to be three raps at our door, and we used to wait for it. We never called "Come in", and it wasn't until quite a long time afterwards, that we saw the nun, I know the date was the 28th July but I can't remember the year. I was walking round the garden with two of my sisters, and they'd been to a garden party and telling me an amusing story that had happened. And then they wondered I didn't take any notice and they looked down at me, and I said "Look there's a nun walking there". And I was terrified and so were they when they saw her – and it sent cold shivers down our backs and we simply flew up to the house. And then we saw my eldest sister who was staying with us and she said "Oh I'm not going to be frightened", so she came down, and when she saw the nun she made to go across the potato bed to meet the nun, and the nun turned and came as it were to meet her, and she was seized with panic and simply flew up to the house. But nothing in the house ever disturbed us.

NARRATOR: The nun was seen and knockings were heard. One of the strangest things about the haunted rectory is the way poltergeists and ghosts are mixed up together. You know what a ghost is? What is a poltergeist? Well, it's supposed to be a mischievous – imp if you like – a force which throws things, breaks things, makes noises – there's no logical reason for what they are alleged to do.

Remember these are the eye-witness accounts of reputable people. But listen to this: as well as the large rectory, the Reverend Henry Bull built stables, out-houses, and a coachhouse with living accommodation above. Hear Mr. and Mrs. Cooper who lived there thirty years ago.

(FADE INTO DISC 8 BAND 3)

MRS. COOPER: We lived there four years, and after we'd been there a little while my husband asked me if I heard noises in the house. I said what sort of noises. He said well something like a large dog overhead. We weren't superstitious or anything or nervy and we've never heard anything. I suggested it might be cats or rats or something like that. So we investigated the loft to see if there was anything that could get through into the roof but there was nothing there because everything was pretty solid there. But one afternoon I did hear a rapping overhead quite loud ones, and then I realised there really was noises and it wasn't imagination. Then after another little while he came in one evening and asked me if I'd seen a Sister of Mercy up there anywhere. And I said "No". He said he saw one when he came from the garden door, he saw a Sister of Mercy and she seemed to come from the back entrance of the Rectory and went towards the road. They thought there was something strange about her movements and followed her about six yards behind but she had completely disappeared when she reached the road. It was dusk at the time, but we thought she was collecting money for some charitable object. Then one night, my husband thought he saw the coach.

DISC 10 BAND 4

MR. COOPER: It was a moonlight evening, I was looking out of the window and I saw in the distance what appeared to be an old fashioned coach, with horses and two headlights, the lights glittering on the harness and the horses, and there was no sound whatever. I called my wife to come and see, but before she arrived it had all disappeared.

DISC 11: But did anything definite happen, Mrs. Cooper, anything tangible?

MRS. COOPER: Yes, the last year we were there, something definite did happen. We'd been in bed some little time, when my husband said "There's something in this room", and immediately there was a tremendous crash as though someone had dropped a heavy tray of crockery all over the table. He wasn't asleep but was just laying still and thought he heard a slight movement at the head of the bed. Then he saw a dark figure go round the bed, which he thought might be a dog. He got a light quickly and it wasn't actually dark at the time – it was about June – he looked through the house everywhere and expected to find all the crockery in the kitchen broken after the crash, but there was nothing touched, it all happened in no time. My daughter was about thirteen then and she was sleeping in another room but she didn't hear a thing. We never found out the cause of the noise, we'd never heard of the Rectory being haunted or any legend connected with it. We left the place in March 1920 and we never told anyone of our experiences there, until 1929 when it was in the papers.

NARRATOR: Oh yes, it appeared in the papers – wonderful copy. The little village which had kept its rumours for so long was suddenly headline news.

(FADE. THEN INTO EFFECT TELEPHONE RINGING)

EDITOR: City desk. Hallo – hallo?

REPORTER: *(distant, distorted)* Chief – Chief? Is that you?

EDITOR: Yeah, go ahead.

REPORTER: I'm down here in a tiny village in Essex. I've got a whale of a story. A haunted rectory.

EDITOR: Haunted? Don't give me that stuff.

REPORTER: I tell you it's haunted. It's been haunted for years. I've seen it myself.

EDITOR: Seen what yourself?

REPORTER: There's a ghostly nun and a coach and footsteps.

EDITOR: What have you seen?

REPORTER: A ghostly light in one of the windows.

EDITOR: *(contemptuously)* A ghostly light! No fairies?

REPORTER: Seriously, Chief. This is terrific. It's got me scared.

EDITOR: You've got me scared you're daffy. Send in your story. D'you want any help?

REPORTER: Can you send me down a ghost-hunter? One of those psychic-research johnnies?

EDITOR: All right, I'll see what I can do. And send in your story.

(BANGS DOWN RECEIVER)

(muttering) Ghosts! What nonsense. *(calling)* Hey Joe. what's the name of that psychic-research investigator?

2ND REPORTER: *(other side of office)* D'you mean Harry Price?

EDITOR: That's him. Get his phone number, will you? I want to talk to him.

HARRY PRICE: When that Editor rang up it was the first intimation I had of the existence of the haunted rectory. For years I had been interested in psychic research, and I gladly accepted his invitation to investigate. I thought then it might occupy my attention for a week or two. Little did I dream that nearly twenty years later I would still be engaged upon what has become the best authenticated case of haunting in the annals of psychical research.

NARRATOR: But before Mr. Price arrived to investigate, what had happened? Let's refresh your memory. In 1926 the Reverend Harry Bull died. The living was offered to twelve clergy, and all of them refused it. Because of the ghosts? – no. Because it was miles from anywhere, because it was much too large and gloomy, because it was cold and difficult to heat, because there was no water supply inside the house; because the upkeep was much too expensive. But at last a rector was found. He and his wife hadn't been there long before they decided that the best way to debunk its ghostly reputation was to invite investigation by competent authorities and so disprove the whole story. So they got in touch with a newspaper and Mr. Harry Price arrived –

(DOOR OPENS AND SHUTS)

RECTOR'S WIFE: And this is the dining-room, Mr. Price.

PRICE: All the rooms are very large, aren't they. No wonder you find it gloomy for just the two of you. And these shutters? Burglar-proof, I imagine. Remarkably large and strong for such a quiet district.

RECTOR'S WIFE: I find the mantelpiece rather interesting. See – this carved marble head of a monk. Another on the other side of the fireplace.

PRICE: Perhaps they gave rise to all these stories about the nun?

RECTOR'S WIFE: Very likely. But I consider it all a lot of nonsense. I simply refuse to believe in ghosts.

PRICE: This large dining-room window. Why is it bricked up?

RECTOR'S WIFE: There are all sorts of stories about it. And one's quite incredible. People say the first rector, the Reverend Henry Bull bricked it up because a spectral nun habitually peered through the window. And he got so annoyed with her looking at them while they were eating that he had it bricked in.

PRICE: Extraordinary. You've never seen her?

RECTOR'S WIFE: Never! But I did find a skull.

PRICE: A skull?

RECTOR'S WIFE: Yes, tied up in a parcel in a cupboard in the library. I untied the brown paper wrappings and there was a skull apparently of a young woman so we discovered, in perfect condition.

PRICE: What did you do with it?

RECTOR'S WIFE: We buried it in the churchyard. What else could we do?

PRICE: Amazing! Anything else?

RECTOR'S WIFE: Noises. You'll hear those yourself. Might be anything of course. One of the maids we brought from London only stayed here two days. She said she saw a shadowy figure leaning over the gate. She was terrified. Wouldn't stay another minute. Packed her bags and off she went.

PRICE: And what about the girl you've got now? She says she's seen things so I hear?

RECTOR'S WIFE: I'll ring for her. You can speak to her yourself.

(*BELL JANGLES IN DISTANCE. PAUSE. THEN DOOR OPENS*)

MARY: You rang, Ma'am?

RECTOR'S WIFE: Yes Mary. This is Mr. Price. He's from London. He'd like to talk to you.

PRICE: I hear you've seen this ghostly coach, Mary?

MARY: Twice, sir. A sort of cab with two bay horses drawing it, it was. The first time it was going down the garden, and two days later I saw it from the road going up the garden. But when I stopped to stare at it, it just disappeared.

PRICE: Did you hear it?

MARY: No sir. Not a sound, just saw it.

PRICE: Anything else?

MARY: No sir. Except a lot of funny noises. Like breaking glass and things.

PRICE: I see.

RECTOR'S WIFE: What would you like us to do to help you?

PRICE: As soon as it's dark, I'm going out to keep watch with that reporter in the garden. You could keep watch perhaps in the study with your husband and my secretary.

RECTOR'S WIFE: I don't think you'll see anything.

(FADE THEN UP INTO MURMUR OF WIND. HOLD BEHIND FOOTSTEPS ON GRAVEL)

REPORTER: Hallo? That you, Mr. Price?

PRICE: Yes. Seen anything yet?

REPORTER: Not a thing. If my Editor could see me now he'd laugh his head off. Getting dark, isn't it. (shivers) This place gives me the creeps.

PRICE: I find it absorbingly interesting. That's supposed to be the Nun's Walk the other side of that low box hedge, isn't it?

REPORTER: Yes. Y'know, the villagers here are pretty certain the place is haunted. Though they won't admit it. They give you a hint then close up like oysters. Frightened of being laughed at, I think. Must say I thought it was haunted myself when I saw that light in the disused wing last night.

47

PRICE: Oh yes – what was that?

REPORTER: A queer light shining out of one of the windows. There was nothing in the room when we investigated. (*PAUSE*) What exactly are these poltergeists, Mr. Price?

PRICE: We don't know. Wish we did. But at first glance this case seems to be a combination of ghosts <u>and</u> poltergeists. A poltergeist is a mischievous entity whose pranks are usually noisy and senseless – stone throwing – furniture moving – bottle-dropping – bell ringing – door locking. That sort of thing. But if we're going to hear anything we'd better keep quiet.

(*THE WIND LIFTS EERILY*)

REPORTER: (*after a pause*) Look! Over there! What's that?

PRICE: Where? Where?

REPORTER: Look! There she is. After her.

(*FOOTSTEPS RUN ACROSS GRAVEL*)

PRICE: (*calling after him*) Hey, wait a minute! Does he think he can catch a ghost!

REPORTER: (*returning, breathless, excited*) Didn't you see something move against the dark background of trees? I swear I did. I couldn't make out any definite shape, but I swear something moved. It disappeared before I reached the spot.

PRICE: Well, it's too dark to see anything now. We'd better go into the house. Come on, this is the way.

(*FOOTSTEPS UP GRAVEL PATH*)

(*DOOR OPENS AND SHUTS*)

REPORTER: We'll go in through the veranda.

(*THERE IS A CRASH AS HALF BRICK FLIES THROUGH THE GLASS ROOF ABOVE THEM*)

PRICE: What the dickens was that?

REPORTER: Look here it is. A half brick. Someone tossed a half brick through the glass roof. Poltergeists?

PRICE: Someone might be in the upper rooms playing tricks on us. I've sealed every room. We can soon find out. Upstairs quickly!

(FEET RACE ACROSS WOODEN FLOOR AND UP STAIRS. PAUSE. THEN DESCEND SLOWLY AND END)

REPORTER: I didn't find a thing, did you?

PRICE: Every room's still sealed. There's not a soul upstairs. Look out!

(THERE IS A CRASH AS GLASS CANDLESTICK SMASHES AT THEIR FEET)

REPORTER: What the devil—! Someone threw it down the stairs. It just missed my head.

PRICE: A coloured glass candlestick! But not a minute ago I saw it standing upstairs on the Blue Room mantelpiece. And I sealed the room. No one's upstairs.

REPORTER: Hey, I'm beginning to get a bit scared about this.

(FADE VOICE THEN FADE IN FOOTSTEPS COMING DOWN STAIRS)

Well, I searched thoroughly this time. I'm certain there's no one in the upper rooms.

PRICE: Right-oh. Now we'll all sit on the stairs in the darkness and see what happens. Ready to turn out the light? Right!

REPORTER: Can't say I care for this very much.

RECTOR'S WIFE: It's very dark, isn't it?

PRICE: Ssh! Quiet everybody.

(A PAUSE. A MOTHBALL TAPS STEP BY STEP DOWN THE STAIRS)

What's that?

REPORTER: Something's coming down the stairs.

PRICE: Sssh!

REPORTER: Oh! Something's hit me on the hand.

PRICE: All right put the light on. There – now what is it?

REPORTER: It's a mothball – look! But why should that hop down the stairs on its own?

RECTOR'S WIFE: Look out, there's more coming.

(STONES RATTLE DOWN STAIRS)

PRICE: Give them to me. Hm, stones. And a bit of slate.

RECTOR'S WIFE: Someone's playing pranks on us.

PRICE: There's no one in those upper rooms.

(BELLS BEGIN TO JANGLE IN THE DISTANCE)

REPORTER: (*nervously*)   Those bells. They're ringing on their own. There's no one near them. I don't like this at all.

PRICE: Don't like it! Why man, it's the most exciting piece of psychic phenomena I've ever encountered.

(THE BELLS PEAK AND FADE)

NARRATOR: Well, that was seventeen years ago. What does the rector's wife believe today?

RECTOR'S WIFE: I still believe pranks were being played. Yes, stones were thrown and when I picked them up they were warm. And once Mary brought me a key which had shot out of a lock, and she said, "Feel this Ma'am – it's hot." Of course people are playing jokes or how could the key be hot.

NARRATOR: Yet a psychic researcher would say that hot stones and hot keys shooting out of locks are typical poltergeists phenomena.

RECTOR'S WIFE: I'll tell you about one other prank. I was in the house one night alone when I heard the drive gates swing open. I took the hurricane lamp and went to the window. There were two lights shining out there in the drive and as I watched them they went out. But I still don't believe it was that coach they talk about. Somebody was playing a trick on me. And not a very pleasant one at that.

NARRATOR: Yes, even in 1929, someone might have been playing tricks. A ghostly coach? Sounds ridiculous, doesn't it? It's not even a human manifestation. And yet the evidence is so strong. Listen to what happened to Mr. Samuel Seal of Bures thirteen years later in 1942.

DISC 13.   1942

MRS. SEAL: Well, I was in the searchlight battery that was stationed at Belchamp Water. I'd been on leave and I was returning from my wife's home, it would be after midnight, when a policeman stopped me and he said – "Who's that?" I told him – I said I'm a Sergeant from Belchamp Water. All right, he says, come here, let's have a look at your lamp. You'd better get that switched a bit lower at any rate, he said. So I switched the light down. He said, "Which way are you going back?" I told him. "Past the Rectory through Borley." "I shouldn't go that way if I were you. I should go through Foxearth." I took no notice of him at any rate, I went my own way past the school, up the hill, I was half way up the hill when I saw two lights coming round the corner, they were coming at a devil of a speed, and I naturally thought it was somebody coasting down the hill with a motor car. These two lights got nearer to me. Suddenly when about a hundred yards away, they switched across the road, it seemed as though they just shot across the road and there was a dark shape following them. So I thought, according to my estimation, they'd gone through the gate that leads into the garden to the rectory. But when I got there, there was no gate that had been opened as the grass was still up by the gate, so I investigated at the hedgeside as I as going up the road, and I was just against the tower where the rectory was burnt out. There was a yelping scream and I dare swear that my hair must have stood on end and it must have left my head and left it a blooming yard. So I just

51

got on my bike and went back home. When I got back there was one of the gunners I think it was Bill Williams. He said, "What's the matter with you, Serg. Have you seen a ghost?" "Talk about seeing one," I said. "I've heard one too." So he said, "Which way did you come back?" So I said, "Well, I've come back through Borley." "Oh," he said, "that place is haunted." I said, "Why didn't you tell me that before I went that way." And that was all there was to it. But I'd never heard anything about the rectory and no one had ever told me about it.

NARRATOR: If we accept this evidence of a coach what does it mean? Has it any connection with the ghostly nun? There's the story of Mr. Herbert Mayes, who lives at the Green not half a mile away from the rectory. He passed the house for years and never saw or heard a thing. Until – one night –

(DISC 7 BAND 3) (*FADE. AND UP INTO*:

MR. HERBERT MAYES: Well, I was riding my bike up the hill towards the church soon after work. This was March 16th, 1939. It was about nine-o'clock and dark, I came almost level with the Rectory gate when suddenly I heard horses' hooves coming towards me. At first I thought it was Mr. Barnes' horse that had got out of his field. It's a narrow lane, and I didn't want to get knocked down in the dark, so I put my bike back into the hedge. The horses got closer and closer, about four I should say all at different trots. I couldn't see any so I swung my bike round into the road but nothing passed me, nothing I could see, only the noise of the hooves and they gradually faded away down the hill. I can tell you I was scared.

NARRATOR: Perhaps you don't believe his story? Yet Mr. Mayes is a countryman. He works in the fields with countrymen. And some of them have sharp, malicious tongues, and they scent out a liar as quickly as they down a pint of ale. But they haven't moved Mr. Mayes. He knows what he's heard. And whether anyone believes him or not is a matter of indifference to him. A ghostly nun? A coach that is seen and not heard, or heard and not seen? It seems so pointless, so stupid, doesn't it? Vague theories were put forward. A nun bricked up in a convent wall for breaking her vows of chastity? A romantic story of ill-fated lovers racing for happiness in a black coach drawn by bay horses? But there was no proof – no evidence that either of these stories were based on fact. In 1930 the Reverend Foyster and Mrs. Marianne Foyster, cousins of the Bulls, took over the living. The Reverend Foyster is dead, Mrs. Foyster has gone to Canada. But here is the account of Lady Whitehouse of Arthur Hall near Sudbury. A friend of theirs. She has given us permission to retell her story.

LADY WHITEHOUSE: I've known Borley Rectory – and the people who lived there – intimately for a great many years. I haven't the slightest doubt that it's haunted. While the Reverend Foyster and his wife Marianne were there between 1930 and 1935, my husband and I often visited them. On many occasions I witnessed the most astonishing happenings – happenings that could only have been produced by supernatural means. The Foysters were quite the bravest couple I ever knew. But several times my husband, Sir George Whitehouse, and myself insisted that they come back to Arthur Hall with us, when things became too bad, and events could become very frightening.

The sort of phenomena I witnessed? Bottles flew across the room. Stones were thrown. Pencilled messages scribbled on scraps of paper fluttered down out of nowhere. On one occasion my gloves and parasol flew across the room. We heard bells ringing. And on another occasion we found the skirting board of a locked and empty room ablaze.

Some years ago Mr. Harry Bull the second rector of Borley told me that one afternoon he looked out of his study window and saw a headless man go by and disappear into the shrubbery. He went out quickly with his spaniel, and the dog stood on the spot where the man disappeared howling.

Of course they should have dug on that spot. That might have solved something. The Rectory is levelled now, and it's a very good thing. The trouble is someone – someday might take it into his head to build another house on the same site and all the horrible occurrences might start all over again.

NARRATOR: Pencilled messages scribbled on scraps of paper fluttered down from out of nowhere. Messages were actually pencilled on the walls. Voices were heard calling softly –

WOMAN: (*whispering*) Marianne – please get help.

NARRATOR: "Marianne please get help." Was that at last a glimpse of coherency in all the bewildering phenomena of the rectory? and then there were other messages: one which said:

WOMAN: Light – mass – prayers. Light – mass – prayers.

NARRATOR: Tricks you can say at once. How does a spirit sharpen a lead pencil, let alone write on a wall. And yet all sorts of eminent people on later visits found pencil scribbles which they could not understand at all. Doctor Joad, for example. Even BBC engineers. What did all these things point to?

DISBELIEVER: (*scornfully*) What do all these things point to! I'd say over-active imaginations. All this pre-supposing – this working out theories on the flimsiest of circumstantial evidence. Before you start proving anything you'd better satisfy me that ghosts do exist. Why you'll be listing table-tappings and seances and planchette boards as evidence next.

NARRATOR: Oh, you place your finger on a sore spot. Or should I say a weak link. Even the most enthusiastic psychic researchers look with doubt at information obtained from these sources. However, Mr. Sidney Glanville who has been interested in the rectory for over ten years has a theory.

MR. GLANVILLE: First of all let me say that, although I have been interested in psychic phenomena for over twenty years, I am not a spiritualist. Until I became interested in the phenomena at the Rectory I had used table tapping or planchette very little. But if you accept the existence of ghosts, apparitions, then surely you must accept their faculty for getting in touch with our world. So this was one of the means we used to get in touch with the entities who manifested themselves at the rectory. The results we obtained seemed to provide us with a clue to the nun's identity and a clue to where her remains might be buried. It seemed obvious that her unhappy spirit was seeking help. By the bye, an analysis of records show that manifestations were strongest when there were women in the rectory. Everything pointed to the restless spirit of a woman seeking escape from what one might call a spiritual imprisonment, into which some event in the past had plunged her. And it was to my daughter that one of these appeals came; it was in October 1937. She had never used planchette before. The pencil wrote the name of Marie Lairre, where she came from, and when she died. Indeed the story which we obtained from long and exhaustive sittings, over a matter of months was this:–

Marie Lairre, a young French nun from a convent at Bures, not far away, was murdered by one of the Waldegrave family in 1667. The Waldegraves were Lords of the Manor in this part of the country for centuries. And as a matter of fact the ornate tomb of a Sir Edward Waldegrave and his wife stands in the little parish church opposite the

	rectory today. Mr. Harry Price agrees with me, I believe. That is so, isn't it, Mr. Price?
PRICE:	Yes, the story is both reasonable and coherent. A young French novice comes from her nunnery at Le Havre; rests for a while at a similar establishment at Bures near the rectory, gets involved with and is removed by one of the young Waldegraves who, for some reason we don't understand, murders her by strangling. The novice – wherever her spirit rests – appeals by means of the manifestations you have heard about for a Christian burial, and being a Roman Catholic wants a requiem mass said for her, incense, holy water and above all prayers. I have just received confirmation from an investigator of mine that Mary Lairre did live in the 17th century, and that she did come to England. I find this circumstantial evidence very strong – I might almost say conclusive.
NARRATOR:	Well, that's one explanation. But let us return to the factual history of the haunted rectory. In October 1935 the Foysters vacated the living. Not because of ghosts, but because Mr. Foyster's health was failing. The ecclesiastical authorities then decided that it was too large and too expensive for the small modern family likely to reside there; the living was incorporated with that of the adjoining parish and in 1936 the Reverend Henning arrived. The house was up for sale. A haunted house for sale for £500 and no one would buy it. It was during this period that Mr. Harry Price rented it for a year and inserted the following advertisement in the Personal Column of The Times –
READER (MALE):	"Haunted House. Responsible persons of leisure and intelligences, intrepid, critical and unbiased, are invited to join rota of observers in a year's night and day investigation of alleged haunted house in Home Counties. House situated in lonely hamlet so own car is essential."

HARRY PRICE: Yes, the result of that advertisement was quite phenomenal. I received letters from people as far removed in the social scale as charwomen – and countesses. One man modestly suggested a salary of ten pounds a week as suitable remuneration. But it was quite a unique arrangement. I selected about forty people of the right type and I got the candid accurate observation I wanted. The following reports are a few of the hundreds I received:-

(WIND UP AND UNDER)

1ST MAN: At about two a.m. we were sitting on the landing in the dark and we heard –

(EFFECT: HEAVY FOOTSTEPS IN DISTANCE)

The footsteps walked across the hall underneath us. There was no mistaking them. There was no one else in the house.

(WIND UP AND UNDER)

2ND MAN: At seven-fifty p.m. I was on watch in the Blue Room. I heard this –

(EFFECT: THREE SHARP KNOCKS)

The house was empty except for myself.

(WIND UP AND UNDER)

3RD MAN: Suddenly the air around me became ice-cold, my hands became icy and in fact I became cold all over and my hair stood on end. I was rigid. The sensation lasted as nearly as I can judge about twenty seconds and then passed off.

(WIND UP AND UNDER)

4TH MAN: We were quietly waiting in the Blue Room at half past midnight when suddenly –

(EFFECT: ELECTRIC BELLS RING LOUDLY)

There was no reason for the electric bell to ring. The switch had been disconnected. It was a very startling experience.

(WIND UP AND UNDER)

KERR-PEARSE: I was sitting in the base room finishing supper when I heard a distinct click. A few seconds later when going to the pantry to wash up, I realised that the click had been caused by the key turning in the lock. The key was on my side of the door. Whatever had locked the door was still in the room with me.

(WIND UP AND UNDER)

NARRATOR: Remember these were critical unbiased researchers. And they're only a few isolated examples of the phenomena experienced. Mr. Price's tenancy ended, and just before the war the house was sold to a Captain Gregson. It was during his stay there that the rectory caught fire. Captain Gregson had quite a time there –

CAPTAIN GREGSON: Well, I always felt that the atmosphere attached to the house was quite foreboding. One only had to stand in the courtyard for a moment and one would sense it. It was so cold and dark and oppressive. Then one evening I was going to draw some water from the pump in the courtyard. I thought I heard footsteps overhead, so I stopped to listen. I had my dog with me and my dog stopped to listen too, and I noticed his hair bristling. Then, all of a sudden, he began to howl. He howled, turned and ran away, and he never came back. We never saw him again. We got a new puppy a few weeks later – didn't want to be without a dog you know – but one evening exactly the same sort of thing happened, and we lost the puppy as well. That's odd enough but it's not the only odd thing about the place, not by a long way. In one of our cellars there was an old well; it's dangerous and it's difficult to see in the dark, in

58

the corner of the cellar, so I had it covered up with a very heavy wooden hatch cover – a great heavy thing weighing a hundredweight or more, but one morning we came down and we found that the hatch had been taken off and thrown clear across the cellar. Then again, another morning, when it had been snowing, we found a set of very queer formless kind of footprints outside in the snow. They led right up to the house and then they ceased and there were no return footsteps – quite a curious thing. Then, listen to this: we caught a hideous old toad in the cellar, we didn't like him much there, so we wrapped him up quite securely in a blue and white teacloth and made a sort of bag of it, tied with a cord around the neck so as to keep him in, but a few minutes afterwards, when we sent to pick him up, we had an idea of taking him away to the garden or fish-pond or somewhere when we went to pick him up he was not there, he had disappeared, and there's no accounting for it at all. He was certainly not in the cellar. Then about the fire; it happened like this; I was sorting books in the library. We were living in the cottage before moving into the Rectory itself. An oil lamp, which in the ordinary way I would have considered perfectly safe, suddenly fell over automatically it seemed, and in a matter of seconds the whole library was ablaze. Of course, we got the Fire Brigade from Sudbury, but it was quite useless – the whole house was ablaze. Then I suppose I really was a little startled when someone who had known nothing at all about the supposed hauntings came to ask me who were the cloaked lady and gentleman who had come out of the Rectory and joined me on the lawn when the fire was at its height. You see, I had been quite alone at the time.

NARRATOR: That was in 1939. The Rectory was destroyed by fire. And today there is not one stone standing upon another. The end of the story? Well let the

Reverend Henning tell of the part he played in what may have been the final denouement.

REVEREND HENNING: By this time several authorities had been puzzling over the wall writings and weighing up the evidence presented by the various phenomena. They deciphered that the pencil scrawlings on the wall not only signified "light, mass, prayers" but also found <u>this</u> cryptic message "Marianne – get help. Well – tank – bottom – me." Together with the planchette messages we felt that this provided sufficient incentive to clear the well in the cellar and excavate the floor there. But it was easier said than done. Remember in the war years it was extremely difficult to get labour. Eventually, however, with the help of an old labourer I started the work myself. Clearing the well we found a silver cream jug of fairly modern design and two religious medallions such as nuns wear. And in one corner of the cellar we made a very interesting find indeed – a piece of human skull and a jawbone. Now what were human remains doing buried in the corner of a rectory cellar? Was this the jawbone of the ghostly nun? Was this a part of the mystery solved? Mr. Price, what do you think?

MR. PRICE: Well, let me tell you what happened after Mr. Henning gave me the bones. I submitted the piece of skull and the jawbone to a first class West End dental surgeon. He expressed the opinion that the skull was that of a youngish person, but that the fragment was too small to determine the sex of the owner. But he expressed the definite opinion that the jawbone belonged to a young woman around the age of thirty. If this was the nun she desired a Christian burial so we re-interned these remains in a neighbouring churchyard. Now! Would this finally end the mysterious hauntings? Would the nun at last rest in peace? Well, it did seem that the poltergeist activity was growing weaker. But of course only the years and more intense research can satisfy our curiosity completely.

NARRATOR: One other small mystery has never been investigated. The seances and planchettes messages had suggested that church plate was buried in the garden. Empting the well had only revealed a jug of comparatively modern design. And inquisitive diviners prospecting the gardens had all discovered at a certain spot that their divining rods indicated a strong reaction to gold. Was it the buried church plate? Burgess and Eton decided to find out. Hard labour would tell them.

ETON: Hard labour is the right description. With the assistance of a local diviner we plotted out the position of the strange underground influence. We enlisted the help of brother producer Rayner Heppenstall as a volunteer digger –

BURGESS: And we dug.

ETON: We dug six feet.

BURGESS: We got blisters.

ETON: We got caustic comments from the local farmhands.

TURNER: The sight of three BBC chaps stripped to the waist and neck-deep in Mother Earth was a sight for sore eyes – a psychic phenomenon of the highest order.

BURGESS: Of course it's not everybody who gets the opportunity of digging for buried treasure.

ETON: It's not everybody who wants it.

BURGESS: A few local enthusiasts took over and they dug.

ETON: Our hole reached the incredible depth of nine feet seven inches.

BURGESS: No treasure?

ETON: No treasure. Not a sausage!

BURGESS: So we gave up.

ETON: Moral: never trust a planchette board!

Perhaps you think our evidence has been on the side of the ghosts? Well, listen for a moment to a man who lived at the Rectory cottage and doesn't believe in ghosts. After Captain Gregson left the Rectory, a contractor levelled the house to the ground, sold the bricks and timber, divided the land into two lots, and sold one to Mr. Russell. This is his opinion . . .

(DISC 18)

MR. RUSSELL: Well, I arrived in early July, left there in April. I was warned about the place being haunted, but that kind of nonsense doesn't matter much to me. I arrived there and I must admit the first night or two I heard rather peculiar noises. I heard tappings on the roof; they turned out to be jackdaws; tappings on the windows and on the chimneys. I saw lights across the meadows; they turned out to be the lights of Sudbury. People used to come at night, especially the night of July 28th; young students who asked to spend the night down beneath the old cedar tree, where there used to be an old summer-house, in order that they could sit there and watch the Nun. Other peculiar people came down, with long black beards, piercing eyes and rather white unpleasant faces. I saw them in the morning, sodden wet through, blue in the face, with their teeth chattering, and all they caught was a cold, and that is all there is to catch.

NARRATOR: The other plot was sold to Mr. Gooch, a farmer, and a native of Borley.

(DISC 1)

MR. GOOCH: I bought half the ground of Borley Rectory on purpose to build a workshop, which I have done, and I intend later on to build a house higher up. There are queer things happening here at the Rectory, such as stones throwing and gates swing open. But that don't worry me, if nothing happened worse than that I can get on with my job. Most things that do bother me is the damned people that get in my way all the time.

NARRATOR: No, the ghosts – if any – didn't worry Mr. Gooch. And a lady down the road – well, she had strong feelings about the matter.

(DISC 4 BAND 2)

MRS. PEARSON   Don't mention the Rectory to me – I've never heard of such nonsense. My sister's girl worked there for four years, but she never heard or saw a thing. I've lived here all my life, and I've never heard or seen anything either. All these people traipsing round at night with torches, shouting and screaming keeping me awake – the whole thing's a lot of nonsense anyway . . . ghosts indeed!

NARRATOR: Today? The haunted Rectory is divided into two plots. Mr. Gooch doesn't bother about the ghosts. He's built a workshop at one end of the ground and intends to build a house later on. Mr. Turner owns the other half of the ground now. What does he think about it? Well, here is . . .

(DISC 3)

MR. TURNER: Well, I'm hardly a good judge. I bought this lovely place from Mr. Russell with the object of raising fruit trees. I have the fruit trees here, and I hope eventually they will bring in a lot of money, since I am also a poet. I suppose being a poet one's reactions ought to be super-sensitive to such a place. I often wonder, if I saw a nun coming towards me, what my reactions to it would be. I think at first I'd be extremely interested, if of course, she started to run towards me like she has been known to do, I hope that I'd let her pass right through me. Afterwards when thinking about her and what I'd actually seen, I should be extremely frightened. But up to date, there's been nothing like that at all. In fact, in all the haunted houses I've been to or lived in there's been a queer atmosphere of peace and quiet. And that is what we have here. I don't think that the poltergeists will continue – their influence I think has died, and gone, and so here we're left with a lovely spot surrounded by trees with peace and quiet and the atmosphere except perhaps for a large number of people who come up here, sober and not sober, is one of utter peace and quiet and happiness.

NARRATOR: And that is the story of the haunted rectory. You can believe it or disbelieve it as you please. We have presented the evidence as clearly as we could. Perhaps the ghost of the nun is laid? Perhaps the spectral coach has disappeared forever. But you never can tell with ghosts, can you.

ANNOUNCER: The programme edited by Alan Burgess, based on material contained in Harry Price's two books, "The End of Borley Rectory" and "The Most Haunted House in England" – with additional material supplied by those who took part in the programme and Mr. Ernest Hardy, Mr. Shaw Jeffrey, Mr. Herbert Mayes, Mrs. Pearson and Lady Whitehouse.

Produced by Peter Eton.

* * * * * *

PART 3

The Anonymous Letter

The Anonymous Letter

[This anonymous letter was sent to the Editor of the "Suffolk Free Press", Sudbury on 10th June 1947 for forwarding to Harry Price. Price established that all the detailed descriptions and references were accurate and factual. He intended to analyse the letter in great detail in his projected Borley III. Already he referred to it as 'another Versailles vision'. Dr Paul Tabori regarded it as 'perhaps the most fantastic story that ever reached Price' who said he felt it had 'the ring of truth'. Or was the whole thing a hoax and an attempt to discover just how much about Borley Price would accept? It is one more Borley puzzle.]

To Mr Price.

Dear Sir, I am not fond of publicity and am writing this adventure of mine, solely to try and help Psychic Research.

I have been for walks through Borley scores of times, as I am a native of Sudbury. I was at home here in the July of 1932, and my married brother came in one Friday morning at 11.30 and said, 'Put that old cooking away and come out in the country for the day! I've a feeling I'd like to go through the five fields and home by the Holgate: I've got a slab of Bourneville here, that will do us until we get back to supper at my house.' So we started down the Croft, over the meadows, past Brundon Hall. We dawdled through the fields, thoroughly enjoying ourselves, listening to the birds etc., so it was 2.30 before we got out on to the high road to Borley. It was a glorious sunny day. We stopped at a field gate on the right, and gossiped to three men on a haystack, and they actually told us they had nothing to grumble about. We talked some time, then stood admiring the cottage garden further along on the left. A woman came to the door, and offered us a nosegay which we refused. We told her we wouldn't spoil her beautiful garden for the world, she smiled and told us she very rarely offered her flowers to anybody, she loved them too much.

A little further along, we looked over a gate, still on the left, into a field of growing corn. The gate was padlocked, the hedges had all been cut as low as possible, but there was a high banked hedge near the bend of the road to the village. After we left the cottage, we never saw a soul, or an animal. I said to my brother, it was almost uncanny not to see a single person, he said, of course the children were all in school, and being such a hot day he reckoned everybody were more or less resting. After passing the village, we stood looking over the low railings and hedge of a well-kept house on the right. The hedge and lawn had been freshly trimmed, and I was saying, what a nice place to live in, in the summer but preferred Sudbury for the winter.

My brother grinned, and taking the slab of chocolate out of his pocket, he tore the outer paper, and at that moment, we heard the thundering of horses hooves. My brother put the chocolate back into his pocket, and we turned quick enough to see a huge coach drawn by four grey and white beautiful horses draw up at the vicarage door. Two servants were on the box, and one jumped down and stood at the horses' heads as they stood pawing ground.

The coach was newly painted in violet, with golden scrolls all around it, almost semi royal. The servants wore grey and white mixture homespun suits with knee breeches, grey silk stockings with black square-toed patent shoes with silver buckles. Three cornered hats of the same material, with a narrow white ruche and a white lozenge on the side, with the coat of arms standing out, one man violet colour and one gold colour etc.

The servants both wore long grey wigs, the ends tied with black satin ribbon in a long curl almost to their waists. Of course I did not get all these particulars at first glance. We saw the vicarage door open, and a manservant opened the coach door, then bowed and stood aside while a young golden-haired lady in her twenties got in, followed by an elderly lady. The young lady was dressed in dove grey thin satin with poke bonnet to match and elbow-length white kid gloves. The older lady was dressed all in black satin. My brother said, 'There must be a pageant somewhere and they are practising for it.'

Then the footman mounted the box, and the horses came out of the gateway full gallop our way. I just stood there. My brother shouted and pulled me. 'Look out H— they'll run you down!' The young lady had her head out of the window, and as I thought, smiling graciously at me. Then just as the horses were almost up to us, my brother shouted at me again. 'For Gods sake hold on to the railings and duck to the ground, the devils are trying to reach you with the whip!' I saw what was happening, and ducked just in time with my hands on the ground, and saw the whip curling and cracking viciously just above my head. The horses were still galloping, and I stood up and shouted to the coachmen – 'How dare you . . .' By this time the coach was only six inches away from us and I was strained against the railing and low hedge of the garden, and had to keep my dress from getting entangled in the wheels. The young lady sat back gesticulating and saying 'tut, tut' and I saw the elderly lady the other end of the coach with her back to the horses looking very bored. There was easily room for five people to sit on either side, but the smell of decay sickened me. I said to my brother, 'It must have been in some coach-house for ages and they only renewed the outside for this pageant. I can't think how those two ladies can survive that stench.' My brother was trembling. He said, 'I thought they would have murdered you. I had some bad times as a sniper in Mespot. But I never felt so bad as I did when that whip curled round you, with that dreadful whistling sound. I can't think how they dared to do it. I don't understand it at all.' I hugged him, he always was my two-and-a-half years younger brother and I told him he needn't worry, as I was always surrounded by angels. He said, 'But you don't seem to realise, I might have been hanged, if you had been strangled, as no one would believe a damn silly tale like that! And look at the disgrace to the family.'

We watched the coach going hell-for-leather, as my brother called it, and we both hoped sincerely it would not meet anybody on the road, as it was so much narrower further on.

Then, just as it should have turned the bend in the road, the whole thing rose in the air just above the high bank and hedge and disintegrated like a gigantic jigsaw puzzle. My brother looked at me and stamped his foot and said, 'I won't believe it.' I answered, 'It's no use saying that M— look at those three legs locked together like the crest of the Isle of Man and look at the cocked hats whirling in the sunshine.' My brother said, 'It's devilish – look at the spokes of that back wheel falling out.' It took something just under five minutes for the whole thing to go up, not in smoke but in a sun haze. Again my brother said, 'It never happened, it has turned the corner and is well on its way to Bulmer or somewhere.' I am five feet six inches and my brother was an inch or so taller, and I said, 'You know quite well you can't see it, and there is nothing to hide our view.' My brother answered, 'Then it's turned into the field.' I said, 'You know quite well there is no room to turn there, and besides the gate is locked.' Then my brother said, 'For Heaven's sake let's get going, it may turn, and it won't miss us a second time.' But I was in no hurry, as I felt quite sure of myself. When we got to the vicarage gate, it was wide open, but my brother looked worried and said, 'You know H— that coach could never have come out of that gateway and left the posts standing, but I can swear I saw it. All the same, let's get on, before something worse happens.'

We did go on, and when we got opposite to Borley Mill, a policeman was standing at the door of the Police Station. My brother said, 'I think we ought to tell him what happened, in case there is an accident somewhere about.' But as I said, the coach must have got as far as Bulmer or Twinstead by then, and others must have seen it. The policeman would probably think we ought to be in Melton. So we went to my brother's house for supper and told his wife. She said she would ask her father who was a local gamekeeper that way, if there was a pageant anywhere around, but of course there wasn't.

A fortnight later, on a Friday evening about six o'clock, my brother came in and said, 'Well H— you can give me tea this time, and I'll tell you what I've been doing today. A kind of Spiritualist chum of mine and I have been over the same ground exactly as you and I went a fortnight ago. We spent a lot of time going through the five fields, and got to the high road about half-past-two; true, we didn't see the men on the haystack, or the woman at her cottage door, but we spoke to quite a few people today. All the same, nothing out of the way happened to us, and my chum thinks we two got caught in the cycle of time, and that what happened to us a fortnight ago, actually happened to us, generations ago. He advised that you keep away from Borley for the future. I told him it would be a very long time before you went there with me again!' Of course, woman-like, I wanted to go again the first opportunity and I was very disappointed to think my brother went without me, but he would not take me again.

What I saw of the coach, it only had the large windows over the doors not at all like the picture in the Free Press. I am not sending you my name or address, but on my honour as a Christian, I have written this exactly as it happened to me.

* * * * * *

Borley Rectory photographed 5th June 1926 with Rev. Harry Bull, his stepdaughter Constance and his wife Ivy. The rector died the following year.

In 1930 a journalist asked Ernest Ambrose to take a picture of Borley Rectory for him. He did so and some months later saw the picture in a Canadian publication with a ghostly nun and coach and horses added!

PART 4

Lucie Meeker
on Harry
Price

Lucie Meeker on Harry Price

[Mrs Lucie Meeker, formerly Miss Lucie Kaye, was the first Secretary and Librarian of Harry Price's National Laboratory of Psychical Research and she worked in close collaboration with him for some five years. This 'off the record' report of Price's introduction to the Borley haunt was sent by Mrs Meeker on 18th September 1951. She called it, "The Ghost that kept Harry Price Awake" and referred to it as evidence of 'the lighter side of psychical research'. Mrs Meeker died 7th May 1955.]

It was the first night we had spent at Borley Rectory, that rambling old house in the tiny Essex village where, rumour had it, there were ghostly goings-on, a headless coachman, a perambulating nun and all the noisy clatter generally associated with poltergeist phenomena.

The Rector, a Mr. Smith, whose physical build, character and faith inspired the confidence usually associated with the Rock of Gibraltar, and his nervous but kindly wife had asked Harry Price down to investigate and, if possible, to dispose of the ghost, which they declared to be a most disturbing nuisance and was frightening their maids away. Their trust in our powers was touching and their helplessness against the mysterious and sometimes terrifying phenomena was akin to a hurt child's cry for assistance. They told us their tale of woe over the lunch table and again at tea and we had in the meantime been over every inch of the house and most of the garden. They had shown us the lovely little church just across the road from the Rectory and also the path in the garden where the ghost of the nun was said to be regularly seen walking to meet her ill-fated lover of 600 years before. They had shown us the Haunted Blue Room, one of the only 5 of 26 rooms they had been able to furnish, and said with some trepidation that 'this would be Mr. Price's bedroom, if he didn't mind.' I caught the eager look in Price's eye and was secretly grateful that nothing quite so awesome had been reserved for me. A nervous woman would not have done as Secretary to the N.L.P.R., but I had my limits! The Rector pointed out to me that he had hung every available holy picture round the room allotted to me, and in my presence prayed God to send his angels to watch over me. I was grateful to him for this, for he was so obviously genuine in his anxiety and I did, in fact, sleep well there – though not for long, as I shall tell you.

My room had none of that cold, depressing atmosphere that was undoubtedly a feature of the Haunted Room, and indeed of most of the rest of the house. (It was not until some time later that the portion of the landing between the top of the staircase and the door of the Haunted Room became known as "the cold spot".)

Earlier in the day when we had first examined the Haunted Room we had been surprised, not to say thoroughly shaken, by our first poltergeist experience in the house. Emerging from The Room we crossed the landing (over the cold spot) and were beginning to descend the staircase, Price being a step behind me, when something hurtled by us and crashed at the foot of the stairs. It had passed within inches of us and at considerable speed, and of course we turned – but there was nothing at all suspicious to be seen. The Rector and his wife emerged from a ground floor room, and upon our going downstairs we found that the object was a coloured glass candlestick – a pair of which we had noticed on the mantelpiece of the Haunted Room a bare minute earlier. We had in fact agreed on their ugliness. They had been placed one at either end of the mantelpiece which, with the door open, was in direct line with our descent down the staircase. As we cleared up the pieces we instinctively apologised to the Smiths! I believe the thought uppermost in both our minds was that had we not made derogatory remarks about it, it might not have hurled itself at us. Anyway, it gave us our first feeling of wholesome respect for the haunt and decided us to concentrate on this particular room.

Towards evening we returned there, and Price looked dubiously at the bed and said that he hadn't noticed anybody saying prayers for him! At about 9 o'clock the Rector produced sandwiches and a thermos flask of coffee against our night's vigil, but hoped that we would not be too nervous to sleep. We thanked him, bade him 'good night' and settled down in the Haunted Room to await anything that might happen.

There was only one armchair, into which I dropped, with the intention of putting my notes into order; Mr. Price sat on the end of the bed and lit his pipe, and we chatted desultorily. From time to time we wandered onto the landing trying to locate odd noises, which, however, appeared of no particular interest. We left the door open; the window was shut and the light (there was of course no electricity) was fitful and depressing. It was very quiet.

After some twenty minutes we heard a distinct knock from near the window. Hushed and tense, we waited – and it came again, a clear definite knock as of a knuckle on wood. I forget which of us reached the window first – we waited there with ears cocked for the next knock. After a moment or two it came – a series of knocks, but to our surprise behind us. We had squeezed in between a dressing table and the window with ears glued to the window pane, but the knocks were coming from the wooden back of the swing mirror attached to the dressing table.

What followed was fantastic. For some hour and a half we held a 'conversation' with the knocks in the manner normally used by Spiritualists (and NOT normally encouraged by psychical researchers, for it presupposes a discarnate intelligence). One tap for "no", two for "doubtful", three for "yes" and the usual spelling out of names, letter by letter, by the requisite number of taps. In this slow, laborious way we first learnt the story of the death of the late rector – a story confirmed in almost every sensational detail during the ensuing months of investigation. Question and slow answer followed each other in rotation – names were spelled out – dates given – the intelligence purporting to be the late rector himself, begging us to help him with regard to his will which in some way was being misinterpreted. Much personal data was given, some of which has never been published or disclosed.

After some 90 minutes, the knocks became faint and unintelligible and both Price and I were exhausted. We ate the sandwiches and decided to call it a day. On leaving him to his haunted bedroom I expressed a hope that he would get some sleep. He appeared exceedingly doubtful about it and muttered something about "this damned room". (This, alone, was unusual for Price seldom swore.) I laughed most heartlessly, I'm afraid, and retired to my doubly "blessed" couch. I was very tired and was soon asleep.

I thought I dreamed – but the dream turned to nightmare and I awoke to see a swaying light at the foot of my bed and a white face above it with enormous eyes! I sat up in a panic – and a sepulchral voice said: "Let's get out of here!" I gathered my scattered and sleepy wits and recognised Price standing in the doorway begging me to drive him to the nearest station to catch a milk train back to town and normality. He looked awful – said he couldn't sleep a wink and had a ghastly head and was generally fed up. (Price suffered badly from bouts of migraine which were apt to turn the skin round the eyes almost black, and it was this effect which I had mistaken for those frightening large eyes.) I asked him what the time was. He said two. I said I thought there would probably be no trains out before about 4.30, and what about waiting another hour. (I <u>did</u> want to go to sleep again so badly.) He quite definitely didn't approve of the idea, but agreed on my promising to get up at 3.30 and give him a lift to Sudbury. I thought it a fiendish hour, but I promised, and he crept back again to his own room. Knowing that I should never be able to wake myself up if I once went to sleep again I lit a candle and tried to read. At 3.20 I got up and dressed and tip-toed along the landing to the Haunted Room. Imagine my utter disgust after my own superhuman efforts to keep awake, to find Price sound asleep! I just stood there and looked at him. Then I turned and crept back to bed, cold and miserable. When next I woke the room was bright with sunshine and the terrors of the night had flown.

Investigations of this kind always seem to follow the same pattern – the early spirit of adventure into the unknown without a thought of fear; and then, on the first signs of anything abnormal, the feeling of tension, the keyed-upness, the watchfulness – then the period of fear, and, as the night wanes on, cold encroaching upon fear, then the gradual descent into exhaustion, and the urgent need of sleep that is really difficult to overcome. That first night we spent at Borley Rectory ran true to form.

* * * * * *

Mrs H.D.E. Bull and five of her daughters, Constance, Dodie, Ethel, Freda and Mabel c. 1900.

The summer house in the garden of Borley Rectory with the Rev. G.E. Smith and Harry Price, 1929.

PART 5

My Chip off the Borley Block

by Montague Elelman

My Chip off the Borley Block

[The late Montague Elelman was a journalist who possessed a piece of charred wood he picked up on a visit to the ruins of Borley Rectory in 1946. He always maintained that odd and inexplicable things continued to happen around it during the nine years he possessed it. This is the script of a broadcast he made and in an accompanying letter in April 1974 when sending me the script he said the remarkable story had the added advantage of being completely true.]

In ghost hunting circles, today is a solemn anniversary. Twenty-four years ago the Borley Rectory, reputedly the most haunted house in England, was burnt to the ground .

Borley. It's a grey word that hangs in the air like a blob of damp mist over a tombstone – and I hope the people of the village of Borley will forgive that remark but – but <u>what</u> people? I visited Borley twice in daylight and saw a total of three.

But if this tiny, remote Essex hamlet is a bit short on population, the fact remains that it achieved international fame because of its ugly, Victorian rectory.

I first heard of it when I was in Africa during the war. The details fascinated me. That's what led eventually to a 17-inch chunk of the Rectory taking up residence with me, and the question that still divides my friends is: was it just a piece of charred oak beam, or was it a real chip off the old block?

The reports alleging that the Rectory was haunted to bursting point began many years ago. It seemed to be not so much a house as a permanent psychic demonstration centre where life was enriched by a phantom nun, voices, footsteps, sobs, odours, frequent showers of assorted hardware, luminous shapes, and the smell of violets in January and frying bacon at 2 a.m. People, we were told, were locked in their room <u>from the inside</u>, awakened by the ringing of disconnected bells and treated to the spectacle of writing appearing on the walls.

Altogether, the sermons at Borley's little church must have been a bit thin. It can't be easy to settle down on a Saturday evening to pen uplifting phrases when you know that at any moment you're likely to stop a fast-moving saucepan.

Shortly after commencing my career as a journalist I thought I'd combine my long-intended pilgrimage with business. So one March day in 1946 I went to Borley with some vague idea of getting a story for one of the London evening papers.

The taxi from Sudbury deposited me in a deserted lane. I was at the entrance to the drive that had once led to the famous Rectory. Now it led only to its ruins – but ruins that were believed as spook-ridden as the house had been.

It was said that after giving due notice, the ghosts had started the fire and then shown off a little by letting themselves be seen strolling casually among the flames. I crunched happily in and around the ruins, looked unsuccessfully for the spot where the temperature was supposed always to be supernaturally lower, and then walked through the village. I interviewed a couple of villagers and later returned to the ruins.

The shadows were thrusting across the lane and it was very still. I suddenly felt uneasy. Sunlit spectres are one thing, but things that lurk in not-so-sunny ruins are another, and now the remains of Borley Rectory looked unpleasantly suitable for lurking-in.

I stayed there just long enough to obtain a souvenir – the piece of oak beam. With this under my arm I marched back down the drive to the gate – which had just receded by several yards – and as I went my spine tingled with the sensation that you get when you feel that you're about to receive a half-brick in the back of the neck.

As a new civilian, I had no house of my own and I was staying at my married sister's in London. No one knew where I had been when, late that evening, I placed the Borley wood on the mantelpiece in my room.

I went downstairs to dinner. From upstairs came the sound of my sister uttering a loud gasp. She came down pale and unsteady and explained that as she had passed the open door of my room she had seen what looked like a black-garbed nun standing motionless in the gloom. Of course, she agreed with everyone, it was a trick of the light. I decided to postpone telling the story of my day.

The long arm of coincidence had been pulled almost out of its socket, but when I told them all about it at breakfast, my sister said how interesting, but with her mind on her shopping-list, and her husband said well-I-never and then dashed for his train. Altogether the effect was something less than a wholesale panic.

A film version of the next night would have shown my sweat-glistening head on the pillow with scudding clouds and wind-tossed trees spread across the picture. That would have been a very inaccurate representation of my dream, which was in Baker Street Underground station with somebody shouting "Borley". How the most haunted house in England got mixed up with the Bakerloo line I don't know. Then the nun glided right up to me. Her skin was like grey-leather. She looked at me with her dead eyes. Then she screamed. At the time I did not appreciate how unflattering that was. I leapt awake, reached for my cigarettes – and there came another loud scream.

I grabbed at my sanity before we parted forever. My sister must've screamed. When I pounded on their door, I awakened her and her husband from a sound sleep.

My brother Mike arrived next day. His business kept him mostly in the Midlands but he was on a brief visit to London and was to have the spare bed in my room. I got him up-to-date on things and his reaction was a series of snorts that meant he wasn't impressed. This time I looked forward to darkness and the programme <u>was</u> entertaining. The weather was mild, but Mike was soon overcome by intense cold. He lay there, his teeth chattering. This lasted for several minutes and then he hissed my name. I switched on the lamp.

Mike is a long lean type with one particularly marked characteristic. He can look more surprised than anyone else I have ever met. One reads of people's eyes popping out and their jaws dropping, but with Mike this really does happen. Just now he was a very very surprised brother indeed. "I wasn't asleep," he said, "and I distinctly heard a voice say 'Sit up'." I felt that Mike was now a full member.

The next night we lay chatting in the dark when, 'click' – our light switched itself on. Mike made an announcement. "I do not believe in ghosts. But I do believe that the sooner you burn that piece of wood the safer we'll be." At 2.30 a.m. we were awakened by a loud, irregular chiming. The house contained no chiming clocks yet the noise was obviously inside. We tottered here and there but couldn't trace it.

A few weeks later I moved into digs in Westcliff-on-Sea, arriving at the cheerful little house on a Friday. Leaving the wood with my other luggage I departed again for a weekend in Surrey. When I returned on Monday evening, my landlord and his wife – a charming middle-aged couple – told me that on Friday and Saturday, they'd been disturbed by a prolonged ringing of their doorbell at 8.00 p.m. No one was there when they answered it. Suspecting jokers, Mr Garnett closed only an inner glass door on Sunday evening. Eight o'clock brought the ringing again and Mr Garnett hastened along the hall – and saw that although the ringing continued, no one was at the front door.

On Monday afternoon, Mrs Garnett was chatting to a neighbour at the door when the neighbour asked who was the darkly clad figure that she'd just glimpsed on the landing above. Mrs Garnett couldn't tell her because she'd believed herself to be alone in the place.

I told them about the wood. Well, it was only fair. "In your suitcase," said Mr Garnett thoughtfully. "Been there all weekend," murmured Mrs Garnett. "You did say," said Mr Garnett "that you were thinking of staying a month or two?" But nothing else strange occurred and eventually the Garnetts enjoyed relating the yarn to their friends.

One weekend I took the wood to my fiancee's people's place in Surrey. I left it downstairs in the spare room and at dawn we were all awakened by shuffling footsteps down below. My father-in-law doesn't believe in the supernatural and you couldn't get him out of bed at that time on a Sunday if Frankenstein himself was in the kitchen reading the Observer.

It was all up to me. I started down, then paused. I decided that if I was going down to the wood today, I'd better not go alone. "All right you intrepid newshound," said the beloved. "I'll come with you." The shuffling stopped as Veronica's feet touched the last stair and mine touched the last stair but three.

It looked as if moving the wood was like shaking up ginger beer, which became all fuss and activity until it settled down again. I soon found myself becoming a huge social success and the party invitations always included the words, "Do bring the wood" – as if I could play a tune on it. I never did take my wood to a party; the idea seemed strangely disrespectful.

My bride finally banned the wood from our London flat, so I yielded to numerous requests to lend it. For some years it was passed from one borrower to another. Few said that nothing had happened. Most told of bedrooms becoming icy in midsummer, of footsteps, and of wives spotting nuns beside the wardrobe. Wishful believing? I don't know, I wasn't there.

Came a time when no one wanted the wood and I took it to my city office. I left it there overnight and the caretaker's daughter – who'd never heard of it – arrived at the flat at the top of the building in no-end of a state. She insisted that voices were coming from my locked, dark office. Then someone told her about the wood and I was asked to get the thing off the premises.

That evening, feeling as if I was planting a bomb in my own home, I slunk in with it wrapped in brown paper. Unseen I popped it into a trunk that we kept in an alcove in the hall. At midnight Veronica came out of the bathroom into the dark hall and asked what I was looking for in the alcove. I didn't hear her because I was in the bedroom and when she looked again the figure that she'd seen standing by the alcove had disappeared.

The in-laws came over on the following afternoon and at ten in the evening father-in-law asked who was it in the hall that kept walking past the partly open door. Veronica suddenly stared at me, "Have you by any chance dared . . .?" My face just couldn't capture the proper expression of hurt innocence and the game was up. Fortunately within 24 hours the wood was once more on loan. I handed it over – and never saw it, or the borrower again.

In the following year, a scholarly report on the Borley Rectory case was published. It concluded that the evidence for paranormal happenings there was negligble and seemed to prove that most of the manifestations were rigged. Well now, you're saying. What about it Elelman? Well, *my* story is true, but I think it includes coincidences – and perhaps it's possible for people themselves to create ghostly sights and happenings out of the stories – false or otherwise – that are in their heads, and for those things to be seen by other people too.

I saw Borley again in 1959. We were touring Britain and with some caution I suggested that we make a detour to the old place. The ruins had gone and a bungalow was being built on the site; the third Borley resident that I'd ever seen was working on it.

I stopped by what must've been one of the last remaining pieces of the Rectory – a wooden gatepost. I paused, my hand over the rough brown wood, then I looked at the gatepost more closely. Was it wanted? Would it dislodge easily? I gave it an experimental shake and immediately became one of the many people who've been hit on the head by something at Borley. It was a book of maps wielded by my wife, and she said: "We are *not* starting that all over again."

* * * * * *

The courtyard of Borley Rectory 1938.
A sketch by Alan Gregson, son of Captain Gregson

A tea party at Borley Rectory in 1930.
Left to right: Marianne Foyster, Mrs Mabel Smith, the Rev. Guy Eric
Smith, Arthur Foyster and his brother the Rev. Lionel A. Foyster.

My friend and Ghost Club Society member Tom Brown on the site of the
haunted Rectory during our first visit to Borley in 1947.

PART 6

My First Visit to Borley in 1947

My First Visit to Borley in 1947

[This is the original report of my first visit to Borley in 1947, accompanied by my friend and Life Member of The Ghost Club Society, Tom Brown. I sent this report to Harry Price, together with a report of an investigation, again with Tom Brown, of an alleged haunting at The Bull, Long Melford. The result was that Harry Price invited me to join his exclusive Ghost Club – maximum 500 members – which I did. My Membership Number was 496.]

Saturday – Sunday May 17th-18th

Present: P.I.T. Brown of Weston and the present writer.

We arrived at The Cottage, Borley Priory (the ecclesiastical authorities insisting on the property now being called Borley Priory instead of Borley Rectory) at 3.00 p.m. on Saturday afternoon and met Mr and Mrs James Turner, the owners of the cottage and grounds. James and Catherine Turner, who had only been at The Cottage for three weeks, told us they had not, so far, witnessed any curious happenings whatsoever. They both remember the Rectory as it was previous to the fire and they had visited the ruins after the fire, spending a night there with the old summer house as their headquarters, but they had witnessed nothing untoward. Tom Brown and I were the first to stay the night in the grounds of the former haunted rectory during the Turners' occupancy.

Mr and Mrs Turner showed us the site of the Rectory and the grounds, as follows:

Nothing is left of the Rectory above the level of the ground, but the foundations have not been disturbed and it is possible to trace the shape of the old Rectory from the line of these foundations. The courtyard area is plainly visible, together with the kitchen passage, the covered passage (the well which stood under the covered passage is still standing and in use, although a motor is now used to drive it, instead of the hand-wheel, which is however still there) and the glass house, remains of which are particularly evident. At the south-east end of the courtyard, where once stood the hall, the library, part of the dining room, the drawing room and the main stairs, under which were the rambling cellars; the remains of all of these have fallen into the cellars and they are now three-parts full of stones, rubble and rubbish. The site of practically the whole of the outside walls of the old rectory can fairly easily be traced. In the days before the Rectory was burnt down there were rose trees growing against the house wall stretching from the glass house to the front of the house and shoots of these are now growing up again. James Turner told us he intended making a sunken garden on the site of Borley Rectory, mainly because he had nothing with which to fill the remainder of the large hole caused by the cellars. He has in fact already commenced building a low brick wall, which looks very effective. The Rev. A.C. Henning (who buried the human remains, found in the well of the Rectory, together with other ancient relics) has suggested that these cellars might be cleared out and explored and dug into (it being remembered that it is possible that Borley Rectory was built on the site of a previous building, possibly a very ancient monastery: some ancient two-inch bricks are still to be found among the debris) but Mr Turner rightly asserts that this would be a terrific job owing to the quantity of rubble that has been thrown into the cellars and it would also be very costly and he doubts whether it would all be worthwhile.

Some of the Nun's Walk has of necessity been dug up. It was originally bordered by a low hedge on each side and that on the south side is still standing. Near the point where the stone wall juts south, the whole of the walk can be traced and it continues bearing north-east, running near the site of the Boundary Stone and up to the Rectory. Turner told us he intends restoring the west part of the walk to its original form; fancy shaped bricks which once bordered the path – the low hedge stops where the walk bears north-west – are strewn on both sides of the walk. He intends doing this, not for sentimental reasons, but because he feels it would make a very pretty walk.

The large summer house (built purposely to face the Nun's Walk) has disappeared and the Turners told us they hoped to build a new one on the site of the old one, again not for sentimental reasons but because it is very obviously the perfect position for a summer house.

The south-east entrance to Hall Lane, (where Fred Cartwright four times saw a sad-faced nun standing, in 1927, when he was on his way to work) is not now used although the original posts are still standing in their original position. The large tree that stood on the west side has been cut down and the large yew hedge has vanished. The land sold with the cottage does not extend west as far as the old cats' cemetery which has now been ploughed up and has disappeared. There are stables on the south side at the end of the high stone wall west of the Rectory site and here, it was agreed, we would make our headquarters for rest, refreshment and shelter, should it rain.

When we had been shown the site of the old Rectory and the former grounds, the new owner suggested that we might like to have a chat with Mr Tom Gooch who owns the remaining south-east part of the original grounds. We were told that Mr Gooch intends erecting a house and other buildings on his land and it will be interesting to see whether the 'nun' objects to part of her walk being built over, for the Nun's Walk commences where Mr Gooch plans to build his house.

We walked down the road to where Mr Gooch was busy putting the roof on a building near the south-east end of his land. He was very busy and not especially communicative although he did say we ought to have been there the previous night and after being assured that we were not from a newspaper and had just left James Turner he did open up enough to accept a cigarette and relate a couple of incidents. He was, he said, at about nine o'clock in the evening of Friday 16th May at work high up on his roof when suddenly, although everything was quiet and there was not a breath of wind, the large wrought-iron gates which he had himself put up, suddenly threw themselves wide open; and some of the protecting wall, (he had built a rough stone and cement wall leading outwards from the gates to the road) fell down, although it had been built some two weeks before. Mr Gooch came down from the roof and showed us how difficult the gates were to open now, although we were told, they opened quite easily the day before. This seemed to us to suggest that the foundations had shifted. We talked a short while longer with Tom Gooch, but as he was very busy and we had a lot we wanted to do ourselves, we left him soon afterwards.

Later in the evening we again walked down to Gooch's land and finding that he had gone home we examined the stones that lay at the side of the road and which had been, we had been told, part of the wall that had fallen down for no apparent reason. I should explain that the wall commenced at the sides of the iron gates and at the same height, about four-feet-six-inches, and came down in a gentle sweep to about a foot high as it curved outwards and ended.

We examined the top edge of the wall and found it smooth and even and the cement between the stones smooth and unbroken; we could find nothing to substantiate Tom Gooch's story that part of the wall had fallen down. [Mr Gooch did not mention this 'phenomenon' during his contribution to "The Haunted Rectory", broadcast on 29th June 1947, although he did state that the gates had opened by themselves.]

We returned to the Rectory site and, with the owners accompanying us, we strolled round the grounds. During the course of this perambulation of the site and grounds of the former haunted Rectory, we noticed a considerable quantity of bell-wire, twisted and muddled, lying about together with some bell-pulls, fixings and fitments and other odds and ends – we even found a cow's skull under a hedge! James Turner mentioned that he was thinking of digging for the lost treasure referred to at various times at seances; he added that he was hoping Tom Gooch would help, and he thought it would be a good idea to dig on both their pieces of ground, especially beneath the Boundary Stone but unfortunately this had disappeared and Turner said he was not even sure of its exact original position although the Rev. Henning had told him that he believed it had been somewhere close against the high stone wall at the west end of the grounds.

After a while the Turners left us to our own devices and my friend and I opened our copy of "The End of Borley Rectory" at the plan of the grounds and, as I had surmised, the Boundary Stone was clearly marked. Using Mr Harry Price's well-drawn plan and by measuring, using the scale of the plan, we arrived at what we felt was very near the spot where the Boundary Stone once stood. Later we pointed this out to Mr Turner and suggested that he dig within a radius of three feet from that spot; he agreed and, I understand, intends to do this. He also said he was not sure of the site of the original summer house, which he had already told us he wanted to rebuild. My friend and I went over to the large tree which stood to the west of the summer house and by comparing the tree with the photograph of the summer house in Harry Price's book, we were able to get the exact angle and so could tell Mr Turner the exact spot where the original summer house stood. Mr Turner suggested, rather obviously we felt, that during the night it might be most profitable to concentrate on the ruins and site of the Rectory, the Nun's Walk and Borley Church.

Borley Church stands just across the road from the north-west entrance to the former Rectory and Turner suggested we concentrate on the church mainly because a recent visitor had said that he had experienced some interesting phenomena in the church, although he would not say exactly what he had seen or heard. I am inclined to think it was this person whom Mr Harry Price later referred to in his "Monday Night at Eight" broadcast when he said footsteps had followed a visitor up the aisle of the church and he had heard the latch of the door rattle although no one was near it.

The Turners also told us of an interesting occurrence at the site of the Rectory only two days before we were there. Mr Peter Eton and Mr Alan Burgess from the BBC, Producer and Editor, had visited the Rectory site that evening and while Peter Eton stood on a concrete slab at one side of the ruins of the Rectory cellars, his colleague stood on the other side and they both heard a number of short sharp raps. Peter Eton then asked the raps to stop and then to recommence and they stopped and continued as he asked. He was very interested and is hoping to make a broadcast from Borley in which the Turners and other local people could take part. [This was "The Haunted Rectory" broadcast on 29 June 1947, six weeks after our visit]

We were most interested to hear that what sounded like paranormal raps had been heard so recently, especially as they now appeared to be one of the main ingredients of the Borley haunting and are what we had though we were most likely to experience among the various phenomena reported at Borley.

The famous 'nun', we were told, had also been seen quite recently but no details were forthcoming, and also the phantom coach, or rather this had been heard but not seen. Apparently a local man, cycling past the Rectory grounds on this way home one evening, heard the galloping of horses' hoofs and the sound of the wheels of a coach coming towards the Rectory site. He dismounted and standing at one side of the road heard, but did not see, the sound of a coach-and-horses dash out of the field on the east side of the church and over the road, making a swishing and creaking sound as it tore past him and disappeared into the former grounds of the Rectory.

Our time at Borley was quickly passing and we thought we would like to visit Liston Church which lies only about one-and-a-half miles north of Borley and see the burial place of the alleged remains of the ghost nun together with the medallion and pendants which mysteriously appeared at Borley and are presumed to have either belonged to the nun or concerned her. The Rev. A.C. Henning, Rector of Borley-cum-Liston had interred these items in 1945.

On the way to Liston Church we passed the vicarage at Liston, but the Rev. Henning was not at home. We decided that one of the first things we should do on our next visit to the Borley district would be to see the Rev. Henning for we had been told that his whole life is Borley although [at that time] he had witnessed little phenomena although of course he will always be associated with the haunting since he buried the human remains found at Borley Rectory, and for helping to find the silver chased and fluted cream jug in the well and other associations. [Subsequently the Rev. A.C. Henning told me of a quantity of apparent phenomena he, his wife, and his two sons had personally experienced, including wall writing, footsteps, unexplained music and movement of objects – incidents that convinced the Hennings of the reality of paranormal activity at Borley and he went on to produce a fascinating booklet entitled "Haunted Borley"]

At Liston Church we were able to locate the approximate spot where the human remains and secular findings were buried, although of course, there is nothing to mark the interment. [Years later attempts were made to locate the casket of human remains but without success.]

We then walked to Long Melford for tea and arrived back at Borley about six p.m. As we walked into the grounds we noticed a car, containing two men, parked at the side of the road opposite to the main Rectory entrance. As we entered the grounds, one of the gentlemen from the car approached to ask whether he and his friend might spend the night in the Rectory grounds. We suggested he approach the owners at the cottage and he went on to say that his companion in the car was a medium and while in a trance a short while earlier, his 'control' had said that if they did stay the night they would be amply rewarded for their trouble, and with no danger to themselves. In view of our slight experiences we later concluded that the medium's 'control' had his dates mixed!

James Turner now joined us and the two gentlemen (while talking the medium himself had joined us) and eventually it was arranged that they would spend a night in June in the grounds. [They did so but did not report any psychic phenomena.]

We next visited Borley Church and churchyard where we saw the graves of the Rev. Henry F. (Harry) Bull, who lived and died at Borley Rectory and is alleged to have haunted the Rectory and grounds – and perhaps still does. Inside the church we saw the imposing tomb of the Waldegraves with effigies of the recumbent Sir Edward Waldegrave (c. 1517 – 61) and Frances his wife with a squirrel, the emblem of thrift, at their feet. [This was later broken off and stolen.] A number of planchette readings and seance messages assert that it was a member of this family who murdered 'Marie Lairre', the ghost nun; others assert that Arabella Waldegrave, the unnamed daughter on the tomb, may have been the ghost nun.

After visiting the church we met Mr and Mrs Payne from Borley Place, next to the church and once the home of the Bull family and we noticed that a false window in Borley Place overlooks the churchyard. We then walked to Borley Green and after a rest returned by a rather circuitous and long route to the Rectory grounds where we arrived just after 9.30 p.m. On our arrival James Turner told us an interesting item regarding Borley Church. As is well known the fire that destroyed the Rectory was, more or less, predicted by planchette and the latest prediction, by the same method, is that Borley Church will be burned down by this September, 1947. [This prediction did not come true and the delightful little church remains to this day to remind us of the many and various actors in the Borley drama.]

Back at the Rectory grounds we set three 'controls' among the Rectory ruins. First, a piece of painted metal, which we thought was probably part of the ornamental veranda of the original Rectory, or possibly the glass house, we placed, as near as we could judge, directly over the famous 'cold spot'. Second, a large curtain-ring, we placed on a piece of cement at approximately the spot where the wall writings had appealed for 'Light, mass and prayers' and finally we composed a rough cross from stones of the Rectory lying about, and placed it on a piece of flat cement approximately over the spot where the human remains were found.

Just after ten o'clock another interested visitor arrived (and in fact unannounced visitors continued to arrive, on foot and in cars, from the time we arrived back at the Rectory grounds that evening until well after 11.30 that night!) and each visitor was patiently shown the grounds by James and Catherine Turner – it was the first of many such evenings for them. One visitor told us he was very interested in Psychic Research and had met Mr Harry Price but he declined to give his name. (!)

From 10.15 p.m. until 11.40 p.m. we sat on one of the old rafters, signed by the Rectory fire, which now lay on the north-east side of the ruins. At 11.05 p.m. we both thought we saw a shadow on the Nun's Walk, almost like a person hurrying along but just as we were about to try a flash photograph, it disappeared; perhaps it was a trick of the light. At 11.40 p.m. James and Catherine Turner very kindly invited us into their cottage for some refreshment. It was beginning to get rather chilly in the garden by now and the coffee, refreshments and the company was very welcome.

We left the Turners for the night just before midnight and after checking our controls and wandering round the Rectory grounds and Borley Church and churchyard, followed most of the time by Fred, the Turners' cat, we retired to the stables until one o'clock when we again walked quietly all round the grounds, had some refreshment that we had brought with us and then settled down to rest. We did not however at any time drop off to sleep but checked the time by luminous watch each quarter of an hour when we checked a particular part of the grounds in turn: the north-west (east end), the north-west (west end), the site of the old summer house, site of drive entrance, etc., until 3.30 p.m. when we patrolled the whole area, checked our controls and then returned to the stables. At 4.30 a.m. we again checked the whole area and also went into the field where the coach-and-horses are alleged to appear, looked round the church, walked down the road and then returned again to the stables, checking things as before until 5.30

a.m. when we yet again walked everywhere round the grounds, checked our controls and wandered about the remains of the Rectory until six o'clock. We then rested until 6.30 a.m. when we finally rose, cleared up, had a last look round, dismantled the controls and finally quitted the grounds at 7.20 a.m.

I must add that we both thought we heard faint footsteps from the direction of the bend in the Nun's Walk at both 3.15 a.m. and again at 3.40 a.m. but nothing was visible on either occasion; however we did have the relevant area entirely and completely under observation from two viewpoints and the sounds continued as we watched. There was certainly nothing visible to account for the sounds which continued for several minutes on each occasion and then ceased as mysteriously as they began. On the second occasion we suddenly flashed a torch (although the whole area was clearly visible in the bright moonlight) but the torchlight revealed nothing and the sounds continued. It was quite an experience to watch a place that is clearly visible and hear distinct, if faint, footfalls at the place you are looking at and without anything visible being responsible. Had we not been scrutinizing the area from two vantage points we might have been inclined to blame Fred but in the circumstances this was impossible.

Although our night in the grounds of what was once known as the most haunted house in England was not very eventful, we found it all exceptionally interesting and we felt indebted to the hospitality and kindness of the charming owners, James and Catherine Turner. [And we remained friends for the rest of their lives.]

* * * * * *

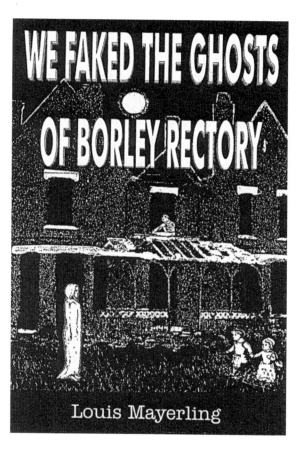

PART 7

The Faker of
Borley

The Faker of Borley

[In the year 2000 a volume appeared called "We Faked the Ghosts of Borley Rectory" by Louis Mayerling in which the author claimed that the whole Borley case was 'merely an ingeniously orchestrated hoax'. The author said he was born in Vienna in 1913 of Amelia Romanov; that he was a child prodigy violinist, a dancer and a jazz pianist; that he knew Marilyn Monroe, George Bernard Shaw and other famous people; that he lived with T.E. Lawrence of Arabia and was driver-companion to the Prince of Wales and Mrs Simpson; that he wrote a prize-winning novel and a musical and that he practised as a medium . . . Here is my full review of the book which I wrote for the Journal of The Ghost Club Society together with a personal interview with 'Louis Mayerling'.]

Is This the End of Borley Rectory? by Peter Underwood

Just when we thought there was nothing more to say about the haunting of Borley Rectory along comes "We Faked the Ghosts of Borley Rectory" by Louis Mayerling which is published by Pen Press Publishers, 39-41 North Road, Islington, London N7 9DP.

The author, who was known as George Carter for the first forty years of his life, claims he spent a great deal of time among the successive families at Borley Rectory, the Bulls, the Foysters and the Smiths, constantly being invited to accept the place as his second home. He also claims to have spent many hours in conversation with Harry Price 'both at the rectory and at his home'. All this is strangely at variance with the writings of Harry Price; Foyster's "Fifteen Months in a Haunted House" or any of his writings; Henning's writings; Trevor Hall's books; Tabori's works (and he was Literary Executor to the Harry Price Estate – as I was – and so had unhindered access to everything); Robert Wood's book; Ivan Banks' book or anywhere else. Nowhere can I find any mention of Louis Mayerling or George Carter. Furthermore over the years I have talked with and corresponded with dozens of people closely connected with this allegedly haunted house: Sidney Glanville, the Coopers, Mabel Smith, four of the Bulls, Trevor Hall,

Marianne Foyster, Harry and Constance Price, the Foyster family, Edwin Whitehouse, the Hennings and many, many other people and no one ever mentioned or even hinted at such a person as this author. Can the truth lie in the author's admission that the book has been 'pieced together from time-stained letters and diaries – supplemented by half-remembered tales and coloured by flash-backs of regressed experiences'?

Just a few pertinent points: 1) The 1900 alleged sighting of the phantom nun is dismissed as due to a servant who plied the sisters with home-made wine; but this was three young ladies returning from a garden party in good light and one of the three ran into the house and fetched another sister who also saw the figure of a nun that then disappeared while watched by the four sisters: that is the evidence of the Bull sisters and family. Elsewhere it is suggested that this could have been a real person! 2) It is suggested that 'newspapermen were always eager for more stories of the haunting' this is supposed to be 1919, when the author would have been six years of age; a story 'extracted from schoolboy diaries' that, it seems, are no longer available. 3) The author talks of dangling a nail on cotton from the small chamber over the front porch and tapping the windows of the kitchen – but the kitchen windows were several rooms away to the left. 4) Mabel Smith is depicted as gullible and accepting as 'supernatural' any odd happening. This is completely contrary to my experience and to available written evidence. 5) There are repeated references to 'hidey-holes', 'secret rooms and cupboards' etc., not mentioned anywhere by investigators, residents or visitors over the years and in "Most Haunted House" (described as 'excellent' and 'dependable' by this author) Harry Price refers to himself and his secretary making 'a minute examination . . . from rafters to cellars . . . measuring every room, passage and piece of furniture . . . sounding the walls for possible cavities or hidey-holes, examining all cupboards . . . under stairways etc.' How could there have been all the secret places the author refers to that Price missed? 6) A few days after leaving the Smiths at Borley Rectory the author tells of receiving a letter from the Smiths telling him that they had left the Rectory; he replied at once and Smith immediately invited him to his last sermon at Borley. The facts are that Smith left Borley Rectory on 14th July 1929 and he preached his final sermon at Borley Church on 20th April 1930 so the account as written in this book does not add up. 7) It is stated that when the ghost nun was mentioned face to face with any of the Bulls they would 'profess a smiling petulance – almost to the point of confessing the tale was a hoax'; nothing is further from the truth; all the Bulls I talked with and their relations the Foysters whom I questioned on the matter replied with a serious and definite assurance that their personal experiences were factual. This, I may say, was to me on my own, to me accompanied by my wife, in the company of Dr Peter Hilton-Rowe, the Rev. John C. Dening and others. 8) Regarding the author's correspondence with Marianne Foyster, he says, 'Each letter was meticulously written . . .' My letters from Marianne over many years were invariably interesting but could hardly be described as 'meticulously written'.

If these items are dubious and flawed – and there is a great deal more – just how much of the book is dependable? So much is so unsatisfactory: on p. 128 it is claimed that Dr C.E.M. Joad visited and met Marianne. My understanding, up to now, has always been that Joad only visited Borley Rectory for one observational period ("Most Haunted House" p. 127) during the Price tenancy in 1937. In "End of Borley Rectory" it is stated unequivocally: 'Dr Joad visited Borley on July 28, 1937' i.e. on one occasion and I recall talking about Borley to Joad and him telling me that he would have given a lot to have met Marianne. Also, although he quotes extensively from purported letters from Marianne in this book, he told Vincent O'Neil some time ago that all Marianne's letters were lost or burned – which is rather convenient. Each reader must decide for himself how much reliance to place on this writer.

Towards the end of this strange book that not only lacks conviction but is proved wildly inaccurate in scores of instances, the author tells of being arrested in Germany as a transvestite and of passing the time telling stories 'and much debate followed my completely fictitious tales of Borley Rectory . . . I became noted for my tales of "hauntings" – wildly exaggerated whenever I felt like it'. What more is there to say?

The author describes his birth in Old Vienna on 4th September 1913 to Amelia Romanov . . . and tells of how at the age of four he was put into the hands of temporary foster parents, Mr and Mrs George Carter of Mayes Road, Wood Green, and adopting their name he was known for the next forty years as George Carter but our investigator Alan Roper has unearthed the birth certificate of George Carter who was born on 4th September 1913 at 63 Mayes Road, Wood Green, his father being James Carter, a kitchen porter, and his mother Amy Carter (formerly Cook); and also a Marriage Certificate of 1953 concerning 'Louis Mayerling (name changed by Deed Poll)'.

Vincent O'Neil, 'son' of Marianne Foyster, is naturally deeply interested in Louis Mayerling and his book. In spite of what Mayerling reportedly told people like Barbara Ecles of "Suffolk Free Press" when he asserted 'I stand by every word I wrote' Vincent O'Neil tells me Louis Mayerling no longer 'stands by every word' and on BBC Television in December 2000 in a programme called The Ghosts of Christmas Past there was a three minute interview with Mayerling and he admitted, 'I have exaggerated here and there'. Later in an E-mail Vincent O'Neil told me 'I no longer believe that Mayerling knew my mother, and if he met her at all, it was only for a brief period of time. As with the other Borley-related memories from his book, the time spent with my mother happened only in his imagination. Unfortunately, he has lived with these false ideas so long, he probably now believes them to be true. There is no credible evidence to support his claims, however'.

Summing up the subject I wrote to Vincent O'Neil: 'Mayerling's book is far, far more fiction than fact. The Harry Price Library at the University of London has no information, and Alan Wesencraft tells me that over 42 years he almost certainly met and conversed with every person who has done any serious investigation of the Borley mystery and he is positive that there was no mention of Mayerling or George Carter. Also, he has examined the files of Harry Price, Mrs Baines, Eric Dingwall and Trevor Hall. This is, I am sure, a novel and should be treated as such'. Borley researcher and Essex resident Edward Babbs said, in "Suffolk Free Press" 25th January 2001, 'Far from Borley Rectory being Mayerling's second home, one has to consider if he ever went there, in view of the glaring errors in his book'; while world famous author and Vice-President of The Ghost Club Society, Colin Wilson said, in the "Daily Mail" dated 3rd January 2001: '. . . it seems fairly clear that the book is intended either as fiction or as a hoax'.

Early in 2001 I succeeded in persuading Lynn Ashman of Pen Press (the vanity publishers) to agree to a personal interview with

'Louis Mayerling'. I prepared a number of questions and asked Ghost Club Society member and former policeman, Stewart P. Evans whether he would interview 'Louis Mayerling' on our behalf. He readily agreed to do so and this is the result together with his covering letter to me.

'20th March 2001. I have at last interviewed Louis Mayerling, on Saturday 17th March last, and have, during the week, composed a report on the interview. I do hope that this will suffice for your purposes.

'I found Mr Mayerling and his wife to be very friendly and inoffensive. He is recovering from an operation and appeared very frail. In these circumstances there was no way that I could have fairly conducted a confrontational interview. He was at pains to state that he would answer questions only on Borley and would not answer anything of a personal nature. Although the questions required were put to him, this was done in a friendly and totally non-aggressive manner, and he made much of the actions of Vincent O'Neil, whom he appeared to feel threatened by. I think that his answers speak for themselves and my interview must be interpreted as being one that you merely have to "read between the lines" to draw your conclusions. Indeed, I think that it was this total lack of aggression and confrontation that caused him to lower his guard somewhat and perhaps say more than he otherwise might have done. You will see there is a reply towards the end of the interview that may well be a Freudian slip that revealed his true nature'.

An Interview with Louis Mayerling by Stewart P. Evans

I have had rather more than a passing interest in the story of Borley Rectory for more than forty years. When the book "We Faked The Ghosts of Borley Rectory" by Louis Mayerling, London, Pen Press, 2000, appeared some months ago it goes without saying that I bought a copy. I am very familiar with the story and I have a large collection of Borley books and related ephemera. I found this new book rather extraordinary and the claims of its author incredible. To call it controversial may be an understatement. The name of the author, so far as I have been able to ascertain, was not known to Borley aficionados before the mid 1990s. But like it or loathe it, the book simply cannot be ignored. The fantastic claims of the author have been strongly challenged, not least of all by

Vincent O'Neil, the adopted son of Marianne Foyster, wife of the Reverend Lionel A. Foyster, Rector of Borley 1930-35,and the most controversial of the Rectory incumbents. My own interest in the story was sparked when, as a schoolboy, I read the books 'The Most Haunted House in England' by Harry Price, London, Longmans Green, 1940, and 'The Haunting of Borley Rectory', by Eric J. Dingwall, Kathleen M. Goldney and Trevor H. Hall, London, Gerald Duckworth, 1956.

Although I do not class myself as a Borley expert of the stature of Peter Underwood, I do like to follow the ongoing story as it unfolds and it was at his request that I found myself going to interview Louis Mayerling on behalf of The Ghost Club Society. With no small measure of anticipation I knocked on the door of the Mayerling's neat terraced Norfolk home a little before 3.00 p.m. on Saturday 17th March 2001. My partner Rosemarie Howell accompanied me. The door was opened and Mr Mayerling's charming and attractive wife Barbara greeted us. Louis himself then appeared and we were cordially ushered into the living room. I explained my mission and told Mr Mayerling that although I had been interested in Borley for a long time I would be putting questions to him on behalf of Peter Underwood and The Ghost Club Society. To my surprise he said, 'Oh, I started The Ghost Club with Eric Dingwall in 1938'. The couple explained that they attended the Spiritualist Church and that Mrs Mayerling had family connections with Chingle Hall, the famous haunted house in Lancashire. After a short introductory conversation I began the interview.

I said that in all the records and writings of Harry Price, Marianne Foyster, Lionel Foyster, the Bulls, the Paynes, Trevor Hall, Dingwall, or anyone else connected with the Rectory there is no mention of him.

He replied, 'How do you know that? You see this is one of Vincent's problems. This has all come through Vincent. The reason was, I presume, well actually George Carter the name I was going under at the time, you probably remember. You see I have mentioned that . . . I went there when I was six, in 1919, and then I went to Leningrad then I came back later. I met Harry Price in about 1929 I think, 1930. He was the grand master, I was an insignificant boy. We were quite friendly but he never really took me seriously. There were lots of reasons he didn't take me seriously . . . about things I'd seen, about things that had happened. But the reason was the family again you see . . . But no, that was one reason. I only had anything to do with Harry on the condition that my name was never mentioned. I think I said that somewhere, there is a George Carter in the second book. He married Helen Glanville. Just another coincidence you get in these psychic matters . . . nothing to do with me nevertheless George Carter'.

I said that Peter Underwood was Literary Executor to the Price Estate for a time and has seen all his records and also seen the private papers of Hall, Dingwall et al . . . also there is no mention to be found of him in the writings or records of Lawrence of Arabia, George Bernard Shaw, Sir Bernard Spilsbury . . .

He interrupted, 'Well they wouldn't know about that seance to start with you see.'

There was some talk of Colin Wilson. I stated that it was said that Dr Joad would have given his left arm to have met Marianne.

Mr Mayerling responded, 'Well he did meet Marianne . . . of course he did . . . he did meet her, he met me as well, and I met Joad later in the BBC studio . . . He said "I wish I never met Lionel, I think it was Lionel, I wish I never had anything to do with Borley", he was dead against it.'

I said, 'You claim to be Louis Mayerling born in Vienna in 1913 of Amelia Romanov etc. . . . how come it's recorded that you were born George Carter at 63 Mayes Road, Wood Green, son of James and Amy Carter?'

'That's right, well that's Vincent again,' he responded.

I said, 'You changed your name by Deed Poll.'

He said, 'I put it in the book, it's all in the book, but Vincent's flashed that round the world. My brother-in-law in Brisbane he came across it and he was horrified . . .'

We then spoke of the photographs of Borley that he had used in his book and he said, 'I've got nothing at all now.'

Regarding Marianne he said, 'He [Vincent] doesn't realise the connection I had with Marianne . . . I mention it briefly in the book but I can't put down the whole connection that we had together, which was purely platonic . . . But I liked her you see . . . you see I was a stranger in the country, they took me in, more or less . . . they were very kind to me.'

I then showed him the photograph in his book captioned Final Deception and he said, 'That is myself, they got the wrong caption when they printed . . . that's ridiculous.'

I then showed the photograph of 'Lionel Foyster and Amelia Romanov' and he said, 'It isn't Lionel Foyster . . . well actually you see this is all due to . . . you see the publishers of the book they thought, well they thought, they said, these pictures are rotten we can't print these . . . but owing to my eyesight I couldn't see them at all they look alright to me, so who those people are I haven't a clue. It's certainly not Lionel, now I can see all this stuff . . . they're bad pictures . . . I know that now.'

I said, 'Have you got any of Marianne's letters from after the fire?'

He said, 'No you see I not only lost her letters, in the shoebox, it was piled up with letters, over the years . . .' It appeared he was referring to those lost in the fire at his place in London.

I then said, 'Where did you get the photos of the Rectory model?'

He replied, 'Well I didn't know it was a model, as far as I can remember I always . . . I didn't know it was a model to start with, if it is a model it is very well camouflaged as a photo . . . When I met Gregson . . . I'm sure he gave me these pictures, he was selling them, sixpence a postcard on his, inside the house . . . I'm pretty sure that's where they came from, but on the other hand I've got an idea that, if it is a model, a physical model you mean don't you? . . . Well I didn't know it was a model, I'm pretty sure, I always seem to have had these pictures with me, and I think they came from Gregson.'

There was some talk of Trevor Hall and he said, 'Well you see it was through Trevor that I've written this book, you see, I've been writing that book since I was about six years old, on and off . . . It was around the Coronation '53 that Trevor Hall came to see me and he'd read something I'd written. He said you know about this, he said in effect you know Marianne don't you then he introduced himself to me as biographer of Harry Price and Marianne Foyster . . . .Anyway I said "yes, I've got a lot of letters from Marianne" and he said "may I look at them?" I said, "Yes I don't want them", they weren't any good to me really, "Get them photographed and bring them back this afternoon" sort of thing, and he did. Except one which I remember was written in the Fargo bus station, just the particular one I wanted to hold on to for various reasons. He kept that one but I didn't realise until a long time afterwards. He took his letters of course he asked permission obviously and said "Yes I can use these". He took the letters away and soon after that, I think it was about '66 the building burnt down and I lost everything . . . Afterwards I thought well, if he's writing a book why can't I? So he really started it. Round about in the sixties I went down to Borley to get the atmosphere again as I think I say in the book. It was all through him. He sent me a lot of stuff, I said "Well, in effect you've got all my stuff if you're writing about Harry Price, not knowing Harry Price . . . Anyway, he gave me a lot of his manuscripts, he said, "I've finished with that lot" and he took a lot of my stuff, well not a lot but certain things from him, but not from Vincent . . ."

We had a rather revealing chat about Harry Price and his pioneering Borley book. I said to him, 'Have you got Price's books?'

He replied, 'I've got the original one, yeah.'

I said, 'Presumably you've read that?'

He replied, 'Yes, I've read that.'

I said, 'I always thought that was a really good read, that book.'

He interrupted, 'It was a good read.'

I continued, '. . . that's what got me interested.'

He finished, 'Yes I know, well it's got an atmosphere of its own.'

I said, 'He was a good writer. Whatever you think of Harry Price he could write a good book and in the late 50's, about 1959, 1960, I read it when I was still at school. And that got me interested.'

He replied, 'Well it got me interested in the first place, yeah.'

Louis Mayerling is a man with many an enthralling tale to tell, he hinted of more to come . . .

He said, 'There's a lot of things I haven't mentioned. I haven't mentioned I worked with Frank Whittle on the jets, on his first jet engine . . . I haven't mentioned that I went to Singapore on a one-man submarine to help blow up the harbour along with two others, they were killed . . .'

I am certain that there is a lot more he hasn't mentioned, an amazingly eventful life, the full story of which he has not yet told.

That is the end of the Stewart Evans interview with Louis Mayerling. To the most casual observer it appears to be full of impossibilities and inaccuracies and it will be noticed that he says it was Harry Price's book (published in 1940) that got him interested in the first place. One might feel that he is condemned out of his own mouth.

* * * * * *

Mr and Mrs Edward Cooper being interviewed for a radio programme.

Louis Mayerling alias George Carter

Borley Rectory and Cottage from the Church Tower 1929.

Left:
The author investigates strange sounds heard inside Borley Church, accompanied by BBC producer Hugh Burnett.

Above:
Harry Price and Dr C.E.M. Joad at a dinner in London

Above:
In the 1950s a young Terry Bacon shows off the 'Face-in-the-wall' that Ethel Bull told the present author she well remembered.

Left:
Mr and Mrs Guy P.J.L'Estrange with Ghost Club Society Member Steuart Kiernander (left).

PART 8

Personal Recollections of Some Borley Witnesses

Personal Recollections of Some Borley Witnesses

Ernest Ambrose

[Ernest Ambrose was organist at Borley Church for sixteen years before the First World War. When I met him, in the company of my wife and Dr Peter Hilton-Rowe, at his home in Sudbury in 1969 he was a sprightly 91 years of age and he lived to be over 94. He recalled for me personalities from the past and times long gone by with considerable ease, just as though they were recent events.]

At the age of eighteen Ernest Ambrose had been invited to become organist at Borley and each Friday evening he would cycle from Melford to Borley for choir practice and the same each Sunday for the services. If the weather was severe, and he could recall roads blocked with snow on many occasions during severe winters, he would make his way across fields sometimes feet deep in snow but fair weather or foul he always managed to arrive about half-an-hour before he was required and sometimes, especially on clear spring days, he would stand beside the church on the hill looking down towards Melford, watching the people making their way from Rodbridge, over the stile and across the field and alongside the hedge. On dark winter evenings the groups of worshippers carried lanterns and he would watch the little lights bobbing along like fire flies. In winter the 'evening service' was held at three o'clock in the afternoon.

Young Ernest Ambrose was always invited to take lunch at the Rectory and on arrival in the mornings he was always given a glass of beer. The Rev. Harry Bull was rector at that time and the young organist came to know the rector well. He heard all about the reputed ghosts, especially the ghost nun, and the whole family spoke about such things in quite matter-of-fact tones. In particular the rector's sisters seemed to have seen the ghost nun on several occasions and when the young organist asked about it they told him what they had seen as if it was the most ordinary thing in the world. They pointed out to him the path bordering the garden where they had seen the ghost walking and when he asked what they felt about it, they said, 'Oh we are quite used to it. It doesn't bother us at all.' They also showed him a window in the Blue Room where the ghost frequently appeared during the last week in July. Ambrose emphasised to me that the Bull sisters all seemed to him to be very sensible and practical women who were not given to exaggeration or emotionalism; nor were they especially interested or inclined to search for evidence of the supernatural. On one occasion the young Ambrose found he had suffered a puncture to his bicycle and immediately one of the Bull sisters mended it for him and seemed to enjoy doing it.

The rector too was a very practical and sensible man although he, like his sisters, accepted completely that they had ghosts and he too had seen the ghost nun on many occasions. We were told that Harry Bull always seemed to need a lot of sleep and during the spring and summer he was often to be found dozing in the summer house in the garden; he claimed he had seen the ghost nun on the lawn many times. On the other hand he was a fit and active man and he was especially fond of the art of boxing. He used to pay local lads to come up to the Rectory and spar with him. Once when the rector was visiting the East End of London he was attacked and set upon by two thugs who probably thought a parson was an easy target but he knocked them both out cold!

Ernest Ambrose told us that he had been attracted to a young housemaid at the Rectory who had heard nothing about any ghosts there but she told her young admirer that as she returned to the Rectory one evening in the semi-darkness she saw a person dressed like a nun or nurse standing by the lower garden gate. When she approached the figure, it suddenly vanished. She was so terrified that she fainted on the spot and left the rector's employment shortly afterwards.

The Rev. Harry Bull told Ambrose that one summer evening he was standing in the church talking to a friend, just after Ambrose had left after the service, when they both heard distinct and loud knocking sounds from outside, near the porch of the church. As they puzzled as to what it could be the knocking sound moved and slowly travelled the whole way round the church. They could find nothing to account for the sound and never heard it again.

The young organist always remembered the occasion when he wanted to speak to the rector about something one evening and he went towards the front door of the Rectory, when he saw a nun or sister of mercy seemingly about to knock on the door so Ambrose went away, telling himself he would see the rector another time. Next day when he saw the rector he told him he had been about to call at the Rectory the previous evening but then saw that he had a visitor. The rector told him no one had called at the Rectory the previous evening. Ambrose then said he thought it was a nun and Harry Bull had immediately said: 'Oh yes, it could well have been the ghost nun, she was very active last night . . .'

Ernest Ambrose was full of fascinating memories of his early associations with Borley Church, Borley Rectory and its occupants, and local people. He came to know Harry Bull very well – 'a rather flamboyant figure' – and he also knew the rector's father, the Rev. H.D.E. Bull and Harry Bull's successor, the Rev. G.E. Smith; their respective wives he knew only slightly.

Years later, long after he had retired from regular organ work although he often helped out at various churches, he did a turn one Sunday on the organ at Cornard and noticed in the congregation Alfred Bull, a brother of Harry, whom he had known quite well years before at Borley. After the service he made himself known to old Alfred Bull, then well over 90. He hesitated for a moment and then being reminded that he was the Ernest Ambrose who had played the organ at Borley some seventy years earlier, Alfred said, 'Oh yes, I do remember you,' then he paused before adding, 'We had a strange organist here this morning and we didn't get on very well with him!'

J. Osborne Harley

[James Osborne Harley lived much of his life at Cavendish within a few miles of Borley and he and his family were friendly with the Bulls and knew all about the reputed haunting of the place. In common with many local people they never had any reason to doubt that curious happenings took place at the red-brick Rectory facing the church. I spent several hours with Mr Harley at his home in Cavendish in September 1952.]

In 1922, when he was a lad of fifteen, Osborne Harley went to stay at Borley Rectory where the rector, the Rev. Harry Bull, gave extended Latin lessons. Already the boy was aware of the stories of ghosts and hauntings but being interested far more than frightened he often joined the rector on interminable ghost watching sessions – and thereby escaped spells of Latin grammar!

Many of these long periods of watching for the ghosts took place in the large summer house facing the Nun's Walk or in the little Gothic summer house at the bottom of the rose garden. In both places they would sit for hours on end, 'in so psychical an atmosphere' as Mr Harley put it to me, 'that every innocent inflection of summer's lovely voice would assume paranormal significance and such normal sounds as distant thunder, the sound of a cart in the nearby farm or a sudden breeze would bring us to our feet in anticipation, suddenly more alert and more vigilant than ever.'

Then there were the hot and sultry nights when the rector would encourage the boy to 'listen, concentrate and try to absorb the atmosphere', the very strange atmosphere that frequently seemed to invade the rambling building. Occasionally Harley told me, he found the atmosphere overwhelming and he would escape into the garden for a while where there was often a feeling of expectancy, as though something was about to happen at any minute, but this feeling was not nearly as suffocating and overwhelming as the psychic atmosphere inside the house; although the rector never seemed to tire of the frequent, strange, distinct and poignant atmosphere within the house and indeed Harley said that judging by the excited look on his face the rector obtained considerable satisfaction from his 'attunement with the spirits' as he called it.

Harry Bull never appeared to be disappointed when the long hours of waiting, either inside the Rectory or outside in the garden, were sterile and unproductive. The sessions were rituals to him that had to be observed and in which, in his mind, he performed some sort of priest-like part. What need did he have of the measuring instruments, the tapes and seals, the cameras and the seances when (I have always remembered Harley's phrase) 'he could hail a spectre as easily as I can hail a friend.'

The Rev. Harry Bull was convinced that the ghost nun was often in and around the Rectory. 'She was extraordinarily active last night,' he would sometimes say. 'I can usually tell.' He spoke with a simplicity and sincerity that brooked no argument.

I asked Mr Harley whether he thought the Rector imagined the activity and presence of the ghost nun or did he (Harley) think the Rectory could well have been truly haunted and the rector was sensitive to such things. Harley told me he really didn't know but there was no doubt that the rector appeared to be much happier in the presence of the purported ghosts than he was in the company of his parishioners. They bored him, or most of them did, whereas the ghosts stimulated him. What he could say about the Rectory, Harley told me, was that except during the watching sessions in the summer houses, he always felt that he was being watched inside the Rectory and followed wherever he went; not by anybody or anything hostile but rather by somebody or some thing who had a more than cursory interest in his movements. It was a curious sensation that he never forgot or experienced elsewhere; it was quite impossible to explain really but it was not at all frightening.

There were things that happened when he was at Borley Rectory that pointed to the place being haunted and he always remembered one night, at about two o'clock in the morning, the large bell in the courtyard rang loudly for several moments and the rector came bursting into his bedroom and seemed to be in a distressed state of mind. The ringing bell – which was very loud – had obviously upset him and he appeared to be trembling and muttering to himself under his breath. 'Did you hear it?' he asked. 'Did you hear it? If you did for goodness sake don't tell anybody. I hate this sort of thing being talked about. Promise me you won't tell anybody . . . it was spectacular, wasn't it?'

When the boy promised the rector not to tell anybody the rector became much calmer. 'Oh good boy, good boy, I'm sure I can trust you. I don't suppose it will happen again . . .' Whereupon it did! Even louder, it seemed, and more violent than on the first occasion. 'That's strange,' the rector said, puzzled. 'I've never known it ring twice in quick succession like that before.'

'Perhaps there is somebody there,' the boy suggested but the rector would have none of that. 'Nonsense, my boy, nonsense; who on earth would come and ring the courtyard bell like that at this time of night? No, it's the nun, she does sometimes. Tell you what, if it rings again I'll rouse the servants; meanwhile no harm done and it's quiet now so go back to sleep.' And he left the room. After the rector had shuffled back to his room the boy lay for a long time hoping the bell would ring again but all was quiet for the rest of the night.

Thinking about it all again Harley said the servants must have heard the bell, it was so loud and pulled with such violence and their bedrooms were situated nearer to the courtyard where the bell hung but they said nothing next day and Harley felt he could not ask them because of his promise to the rector.

One evening, as they were putting away their text books, the talk turned to ghosts (as it often did!) and the Rev. Harry Bull said that if after his death he was dissatisfied with his successor, he would make his displeasure felt in an unusual and unmistakable way – 'no footsteps or bell-ringing and anything like that', he said. 'I'll make my presence felt in some really different way – I know, I'll throw mothballs about! How about that? Mothballs, then you'll know it's me!' Years later, after Harry Bull was long dead and buried, Harley read in a newspaper that in June 1929 some investigators had arrived at the deserted Rectory and when they opened the front door they were met by a shower of mothballs! 'Well, dear old Harry Bull always was a man of his word' commented Osborne Harley adding another descriptive phrase that I have never forgotten. 'You know he really was a puckish, lovable man . . .' Harley said he never remembered Harry Bull without thinking of cats. He adored them and they must have ranked close to the ghosts in his affections. He had dozens, Harley once counted thirty, but the rector knew every one and called each of them by name and they used to follow him about putting one in mind of the Pied Piper! Counting the strays that he never turned away but always took compassion on, he had at least twenty most of the time he was at Borley Rectory, Harley told me. So his memories of 'the most haunted house in England' comprised a kindly rector talking to his dozens of cats amid an atmosphere of ghosts and mysterious ringing bells.

Guy P.J. L'Estrange

[Guy L'Estrange was a local figure of some standing being a town councillor, a county councillor and a Justice of the Peace as well as holding other responsible positions. He was also a medium and a member of the Marks Tey Spiritualist Circle. He visited Borley Rectory once, during the incumbency of the Rev. Lionel Foyster, and I visited him and his wife at their home in Bungay, Suffolk in the company of my wife and Ghost Club Society Life Member Steuart Kiernander on 23rd August 1969.]

It was in January 1932 that charming Guy L'Estrange, a cheerful and knowledgeable man of substance, spent the best part of a night at haunted Borley Rectory, during the occupancy of Lionel and Marianne Foyster; no one else being resident at the time, apart from one maid. Learning of his interest in haunted houses Foyster had invited him to visit and give his opinion of the phenomena being experienced. L'Estrange arrived during the afternoon accompanied by some fellow members of the Marks Tey Spiritualists including Captain V.M. Deane (whom I had the pleasure of meeting at Harry Price's Ghost Club in London in 1948). After the rest of the party left L'Estrange had the rector and his wife ('a bubbling, attractive lady') and the Rectory to himself until the early morning of January 24th when his companions returned for him. It was a night he never forgot.

Even before he entered the Rectory he saw a tall figure, like a man in ecclesiastical attire, near the porch – a figure that suddenly vanished when he approached and did not reappear when he returned to his original position which he did at once in order to establish that it had not been a trick of the light or some sort of reflection or shadow that he had seen. Later, being entertained by the rector and his wife, he heard for the first time of mysterious forms, male and female, being seen inside and outside the house; of lights in unoccupied rooms; of articles appearing and being thrown; of fires breaking out; of mysterious whisperings and unexplained writings on walls and scraps of paper. Once, the rector told him, he was working alone in his study when he saw a pencil rise from the desk and scrawl words on the wall in front of him – no hand was visible!

As they talked a loud crash sounded in the hall. Jumping up L'Estrange opened the door and found the floor outside littered with broken crockery. The rector at his side, viewed the wreckage with interest. 'These things came from the kitchen dresser,' he said. 'You can see how impossible it would be for anyone to fling them down here and get out of sight so quickly – even if there was anyone in the house other than ourselves and Mary.' Whereupon Mary the maid came slowly down the stairs to see what all the noise was about; she had been in her room. Shortly afterwards an appalling series of crashing sounds took them back to the hall. When they opened the door an astonishing sight met their eyes: bottles were being hurled about in all directions although no human person was to be seen and the other doors leading into the hall were closed. L'Estrange and the Foysters stood and watched as bottles would suddenly appear in mid-air, then hurtle through space and smash to pieces on the floor or against a wall. 'One large wine bottle missed my left ear by about an inch,' L'Estrange told us. The rector said empty bottles were stored in a shed outside but there was no way they could get inside the house, the shed door was locked and the window bolted.

During a tour of the whole house L'Estrange was told that one room was especially haunted and a friend sleeping there had awakened to see a white figure standing at the foot of the bed. Thinking it was some sort of private joke, he sprang up and made a grab at the form. His hands went right through the thing, whatever it was. L'Estrange said he would like to spend the night in that room and the rector and his wife agreed.

As the three descended the stairs there was a loud ringing of bells from downstairs. The rector beckoned L'Estrange to his side and leaning over they could see the thirty bells in the kitchen passage clanging wildly by themselves. The rector said that the wires of all but three of the bells had been cut in an effort to stop the ringing but it had no effect. The bell-ringing continued for some little time. As L'Estrange stood beneath the clanging bells he looked up at them and said, 'If some invisible person is present and can hear these words, please stop the ringing for a moment.' Instantly every bell became silent.

Later, while alone in the drawing-room, L'Estrange was making notes of the evening's events when he heard cautious but distinct footsteps apparently enter the room. He told us he felt a chill run down his spine but he did not turn round. He heard the footsteps approach him and then pause, seemingly directly behind him and close to the settee on which he sat. He turned quietly but there was nobody there and nothing to account for the sound of footsteps. Then he heard the sounds recommence and as he watched the empty area he followed the direction of the footsteps as they passed on and seemed to go through the wall at the far end of the room. Discussing the matter later with Lionel Foyster he learned that there had once been a doorway in that part of the wall. L'Estrange told us the footsteps were very definite and he was adamant that there was no question of them originating in the room above or anything like that and, although there was a roaring fire in the room, he felt a distinct chill while the footsteps were in the room and especially when they were close to him, just behind the settee.

Other incidents during what L'Estrange always referred to as 'that eventful and exciting night' included the sound of laboured breathing on the main stairs when L'Estrange was talking to Marianne Foyster in the dark hall. They both stood listening to the curious and rather frightening sounds for perhaps half a minute and then L'Estrange flashed his torch in the direction of the sounds. There was nothing to be seen; the dark stairs were deserted and the sounds ceased immediately, nor did they resume when the torch was switched off.

Later, deep into the night, when L'Estrange was occupying the bedroom he had requested, the so-called 'haunted bedroom', he found himself awake in the small hours and immediately noticed that there seemed to be a definite chill in the air. As his eyes became accustomed to the darkness he became aware of a vague and slightly luminous form beside his bed. As he watched the form or patch of luminosity become larger and larger and more dense until it seemed to represent the shape of a human being in long robes, although no features or even limbs were discernible. Raising himself in the bed L'Estrange addressed the figure but there was no reply. Still speaking and asking whether he could help in any way, L'Estrange made to approach the figure when he had a curious feeling that an attempt was being made to push him away. He resisted but found that it took considerable willpower and persistence to simply stay where he was. Summoning up all the strength of mind he could to repel the adverse effects the form now seemed to have, L'Estrange was beginning to feel that he could not last out much longer when suddenly the apparition, or whatever it was, quickly faded and disappeared. The atmosphere in the room lightened, the icy chill disappeared and L'Estrange sank back exhausted on the bed. Shortly afterwards, realising that sleep was out of the question, he quietly got up and made his way to the deserted Blue Room where he sat in a chair resting.

Soon after one o'clock in the morning he saw Marianne Foyster pass the open door. She seemed to glide rather than walk and she wore a diaphanous night-dress which reached to the ground. When he asked her where she was going she replied, 'To – make – some – tea' very slowly, almost trance-like and when he asked her whether she was alright, she replied again, 'To – make – some – tea' and went on her way. Unknown to her L'Estrange quietly followed her and when she passed her husband's room, the door opened and he came out and was very annoyed at her walking about dressed as she was.

Not very long after this L'Estrange's Marks Tey friends returned to pick him up. Marianne came down (suitably attired) at three o'clock in the morning and said her husband was busy writing his sermon for the next day and could they now leave the house please. They had no alternative and they all left.

Guy L'Estrange said he thought Marianne was very highly strung. He was alone with her for some time and she opened her heart to him and told him things he would never repeat to anyone. Once, during his visit, Marianne seemed to have a fit of hysterics – laughing and crying together. She recovered after a while. Her husband took no notice so L'Estrange did nothing either.

Altogether Guy L'Estrange told us it really had been a night to remember. Bottles materialized and smashed by themselves; china transported itself from the floor below and smashed itself to pieces; bells rang without any wires to pull them; there were inexplicable sounds – footsteps and breathing; apparitional forms: one luminous and one dark; and distinct changes in temperature.

Among the most remarkable incidents must be the apparent materialization of bottles and Captain V.M. Deane gave me confirmation of this incredible manifestation when I talked to him in London. He told me that he had cross-examined the witnesses for hours on end and there was no shadow of doubt that in good light bottles materialized from nowhere and smashed themselves to pieces in full view of several eye-witnesses who handled the seemingly apported objects. During the course of a long interview, also in London and subsequently confirmed in writing, Dom Richard Whitehouse told me that the materialization of bottles was just one of the outstanding experiences he had had at Borley Rectory which he visited many times during the Foyster occupancy since his parents Sir George and Lady Whitehouse lived nearby at Arthur Hall, Sudbury.

Guy L'Estrange wrote to me at some length about the way the SPR authors treated him in their critical Report. Certain paragraphs were quite untrue and libellous and, eventually, the three authors, Dingwell, Goldney and Hall, had to publish a retraction.

Guy P.J. L'Estrange JP told us he felt his visit and that of the Marks Tey Circle had gone some way to bringing peace to the haunted house and indeed a week after the visit the Rev. Lionel Foyster wrote to thank him, saying there had been no more disturbances and that there was 'quite a different feeling throughout the house'. Three years later he wrote to say 'the house is now perfectly normal'. But of course things did not stay that way.

The Rev. Clive Luget

[The Rev. Clive Luget was Rector of Middleton, Essex, a tiny village one mile south of Sudbury in Suffolk. During the 1930s and 1940s he visited Borley Rectory many times. He was fond of gardening and built a flower-bordered path leading to his rectory of which he was inordinately fond – so doting, it seems that after his death his ghost was reportedly seen on the pathway. Ghost Club Society Life Member Tom Brown and I visited the Rev. Clive Luget at his home in 1948.]

The Rev. Clive Luget, a rather lonely man who believed he had been visited by the Virgin Mary, first visited Borley Rectory at the invitation of his neighbour the Rev. Lionel Foyster, 'a gentle and charming man' who was worried that the ghosts, which he had heard all about from his relatives the Bulls in 1895, would affect his young, bright and vivacious wife, the enigmatic Marianne.

Clive Luget told us he had visited scores of haunted houses but had never encountered anything like Borley Rectory. On his first and subsequent visits he personally saw the famous ghost nun, heard music and singing from empty rooms (the only occupants at the time were gathered together in one room with him), witnessed the appearance of pencilled messages that could not possibly have been produced by any human being, since he had examined the room minutely and was about to leave the room when he thought he heard a sound behind him and turning round he found a sheet of paper in the middle of the room, a sheet of paper that had on it a pencilled 'Marianne' in letters about three inches high. On another occasion he witnessed the levitation of a pencil and an empty bottle apported from nowhere.

Once, having made a tour of the Rectory with Marianne and Lionel, they were leaving the Blue Room when they all looked at each other as they heard a scribbling sound from the room behind them. Turning they were just in time to see a pencil drop to the floor and on the wall, in letters two or three inches tall, a message asked for prayers. They all immediately dropped to their knees and prayed and nothing further happened on that visit.

Once, in the company of Marianne, as they were walking along an upstairs corridor, they both saw the figure of a man in a plum-coloured dressing-gown come out of a room ahead of them and then, as they watched, the figure completely disappeared. Mrs Payne of Borley Place, called later that afternoon. Marianne knew that she had been friendly with the Bull family for years and ventured to ask whether the late Rev. Harry Bull had possessed a plum-coloured dressing-gown. Mrs Payne replied, 'Yes, indeed, he almost lived in it – but how on earth did you know that?' She was not enlightened.

Clive Luget told us he had also witnessed stone throwing at Borley Rectory. At that time there was a young adopted child in the house, but the child was being fed in the kitchen and Luget and Lionel Foyster had been visiting the chapel on the first floor and had just descended the main stairway when they were pelted with a handful of pebbles that came down the stairs after them. Immediate investigation failed to reveal any possible explanation.

Once too, not long before the Foysters left, Clive Luget was at the Rectory one evening and they were all enjoying a meal when they smelt burning. Marianne rushed upstairs to ensure that the child was alright while Luget left Lionel, who had difficulty in moving by this time, and traced the burning smell to the kitchen passage but could find nothing to account for it and no sign of smoke or the smell of smoke in the pantry, sewing room, the kitchen or the nearby cupboard. It seemed to be localised but without any origin.

The Rev. Clive Luget seemed to us to be a remote and lonely man, and a somewhat odd individual, kind and thoughtful but one moment talking of the Virgin Mary visiting him and the next completely rational and talking about flowers and his friends at Borley. He told us he had visited Borley Rectory on many occasions and always enjoyed discussing theology with Lionel Foyster. Marianne he found delightful, always cheerful and charming and an excellent hostess. He said she brought a touch of lightness and merriment to the rather sombre Rectory. He could not understand why she was not more popular in the village but thought it might be due to narrowmindedness at their rector, a member of the Bull family they had long revered, being married to a much younger woman and in some cases 'just plain envy'. Luget told us Marianne never seemed frightened by the odd happenings that took place almost daily but rather she was interested and sought for an explanation. She was very protective of the children and appreciated being the centre of attention; most callers simply wanting to see the rector. She was very attentive to him too. The only times Luget saw her show any anxiety was when there were signs of fire or when very loud noises echoed through the Rectory; then she would rush about making sure any children in the house were alright and not frightened. He said she had a flirtatious side to her character but this often helped with visitors and local people who called to see the rector but it was exaggerated and not understood by some villagers. Lionel Foyster was essentially a shy and quiet man and Marianne was a considerable contrast but an important help to him, it seemed to Clive Luget.

We were told that nobody seemed to be sceptical of the ghosts at Borley Rectory. The servants, neighbours and everyone connected with the church and indeed most of the village seemed to accept the ghostly experiences of the rector, his wife, his family – various Bulls and Foysters who were often at the Rectory when Clive Luget visited – everyone without exception, he found, subscribed to the opinion that the house had long been haunted although no one seemed especially interested. Lionel used to write up the happenings as they occurred and send his 'newsletter' round the family and again the strange happenings were accepted without question, certainly as far as the Rector of Middleton knew; probably because ghostly appearances and odd happenings had been going on, or had been reported to be going on, for so long, back to the days of 'Grandpa' Henry Bull at least.

Once Clive Luget took a brother clergyman with him to Borley Rectory and together they went over the house with incense and holy water obtained specially from the Well of Our Lady of Walsingham, attempting a mild form of exorcism, and when this had no effect, they performed an elaborate exorcism rite, followed by complete fumigation of the house with creosote. Next day they enlisted the help of two clergymen friends and the four priests sprinkled holy water, blessed the house from top to bottom and prayed and exorcized every room – but even all that had little effect.

The Rev. Clive Luget was certainly a complex man. He was also a kind and thoughtful man who tried to help the successive inhabitants of Borley Rectory with their ghosts and perhaps his greatest asset was his ability to completely accept ghostly appearances, paranormal happenings and the whole atmosphere of a haunted house because of his own experiences which coloured and influenced his life – and death and afterlife.

James and Catherine Turner

[James and Cathy Turner bought the Rectory cottage, the site of the haunted Rectory garden, including the Nun's Walk, in April 1947 and they stayed until June 1950, only leaving, as they were wont to say, because of the constant stream of sightseers at all times of the day and night, and certainly not for any psychic reason. In actual fact it is evident from what they told me and from what James wrote in his autobiographical volume "Sometimes into England" (1970) that the reasons were almost entirely financial.]

James and Cathy Turner and my wife and I were friends from my first visit to Borley in 1947 for the rest of their lives. James died in 1975 and Cathy in 1992. We visited them in their various homes in Essex, Suffolk and Cornwall and they visited us at Richmond, Twickenham and Hampshire.

James, in particular, was inclined to suggest that nothing of a possibly paranormal nature had happened during their three years at Borley and in his second volume of autobiography, "Sometimes into England" published in 1970 (he kindly presented Joyce and I with an inscribed copy) he says 'I never saw anything of a ghostly nature . . . I did hear voices (it may well have been the wind in the trees, although the day was calm) . . . I am inclined, now, to think that they were the noise of aeroplanes warming up on a distant aerodrome' and 'Tom [Gooch] like me, did not believe in the ghostly records of Borley Rectory' . . . 'quite three-quarters – if not more – of the stories told about the house have no foundation in fact . . . they are pleasant whimsy . . .' and so on but he did include a letter from me, as an Appendix to his book, in which I sought to put matters into some kind of context.

By the time he came to edit "Stella C", published in 1973, James seems to have somewhat modified his opinions and in his Introduction to that work he tells of meeting Harry Price, 'a very vital man, a very kind man and one who knew definitely what he was talking about . . . bald-headed, short and stocky . . . with much energy. The feature which struck you most was his eyes. They tended to look through you; they tended, at first, to be suspicious of you, as if he were uncertain whether you were a mocker or a believer. I was neither . . . before we parted he came to understand that I regarded him and his work not only seriously but of importance . . .'

Elsewhere in that Introduction he says, 'I came to know Miss Ethel Bull very well indeed while I lived at Borley and heard her tell the story of what had happened so long ago many times. It never varied. I am convinced that she saw what she said she and her sisters saw.'

There is no shadow of doubt that things were not quite as readily or as easily explained as James sometimes suggested in his books (he also wrote a fictional satire "My Life with Borley Rectory" published in 1950) and fortunately I was in more or less constant contact with the Turners while they were at Borley and they were good enough to let me know, usually in writing, of any odd happening and these letters are still extant. Furthermore not long before her death Cathy gave me James's unpublished manuscripts and diaries. I paraphrase and quote from his writings and letters.

2nd November 1947 James mentions 'a somewhat alarming experience' in Borley churchyard. Strolling over there soon after midnight he sat on the step of the priests' door for about three-quarters of an hour and he remembered hearing Sudbury Church clock strike one when he became aware of something coming up the main path towards him. He saw nothing but plainly heard 'something or somebody with a lame leg and a swishing skirt' pass along the path towards the church porch. He was more than a little relieved to hear the footsteps go towards the porch and not turn down the path towards him! [Mr Turner referred to this incident, which had a considerable impact on him, while appearing in the Borley episode of a short feature film, Spotlight on Spooks, made by Rayart Pictures and released in the autumn of 1951.] On another occasion James told me he noticed a strong smell of incense in the church during evensong. The smell was sufficiently strong to make him look towards the vestry to see whether any preparations were being made for the use of incense. Needless to say no such preparations were being made.

In December 1947 James and Catherine agreed to a re-enactment of the Borley Nun's story by an amateur dramatic group directed by a Mr Sheppard. A lengthy report of the event appeared in the London "Evening Standard". The actors 'stage' was to be the actual Nun's Walk and at the end of the performance, based on information in Harry Price's books, the actress impersonating the Nun, in full habit, walked along the haunted path in moonlight hoping the 'someone or some thing' would materialize and follow her, but all to no avail. The chalice used in the play, specially made for the purpose, was presented to the Turners at the end of the evening and thirty years later Cathy Turner presented this little relic of the Borley story to me.

In May 1947, when I visited Borley with Tom Brown, James told us about my old friend Peter Eton, the BBC producer, visiting the site with Alan Burgess and recording interviews for the broadcast, The Haunted Rectory, aired on Sunday 29th June 1947. Only two days before our visit Peter Eton had stood on a concrete slab at one side of the Rectory ruins while Alan Burgess stood on the opposite side, facing him, and they heard a number of short, sharp raps. Mr Eton asked the raps to stop and recommence and they continued and stopped as he asked. This occurred in full daylight and a reproduction of the sounds was included in the broadcast.

During the time they were helping with excavations in the church on Whit Monday, 26th May 1947, several odd happenings took place. James Turner, the Rector the Rev. A.C. Henning and his wife all told me they heard distinct footsteps and the sound of muffled talking from inside the church while they were in the porch and about to enter the church. They stopped and listened for several seconds and then quietly opened the door but as soon as the door began to open the sounds ceased instantly and needless to say the church was completely devoid of any human being.

The next day while at breakfast both James and Cathy Turner were astonished to hear a loud noise from the upper rooms of their cottage. Really loud and extended, almost like heavy furniture being shifted, the Turners looked at each other, very puzzled, and then James ran up the stairs but the noise ceased and nothing had been moved and they found no explanation for the noise. They told me all the doors were closed, as they had been previous to the disturbance. Interestingly enough some of the upstairs doors in the cottage originally belonged to the old Rectory.

At the end of May and the beginning of June 1947, for over a fortnight, James was busy clearing brambles and rubbish from the Nun's Walk and beyond. This incident has already been mentioned but it is interesting to read Turner's account of the happening at the time. 'Working with a sickle and mostly in the evenings,' he wrote to me. 'I found the same thing occurred each evening as I broke through into the old orchard: the sound of laughter and chattering came to me clearly, yet indistinctly for no words were distinguishable. The voices came from the direction of the Rectory site and always as I laid down the sickle to listen, they died away. Sometimes I called Cathy and she too, as I worked, bringing to light the old path which had been hidden for so long, would hear the voices – but always, as soon as I stopped work and laid down the sickle, the voices, happy and laughing, fled before me. I never had any fear of the voices, only a sensation of delight. After the work was done and the path cleared, Cathy and I would go to the orchard to listen, but we never heard the voices again.'

During July 1947 James Turner decided, with the help of his friend Tommy Frankland, to dig into the well in the cellar of the old Rectory. Tommy Frankland was a Company Director much interested in psychic activity; he was also associated with the Rev. Dr George MacLeod's Iona Community and was a dedicated, experienced and knowledgeable investigator of paranormal activity. Tommy and I talked of ghosts and ghostly happenings at his London flat in Cadogan Place and at my London Club; he visited Joyce and I at our Richmond home and was always ready to put his Rolls Royce at my disposal. He introduced me to a remarkable haunting in the Cotswolds – but that is another story. I also enjoyed several visits to Borley and Langenhoe in the company of delightful Tommy Frankland, who died far too young. He and James Turner discovered the opening of the well after shifting a great deal of rubble late one Saturday night and there was 'a great escape of gas'. Next day the well was excavated to its full depth, some six feet, and the brick sides and bottom were broken into. The digging into the hard clay took many hours but no bones or other objects of interest were found and the whole cellar area was subsequently filled in and planted with rose bushes. A brick path was laid across the centre.

On 9th June 1948 James and Cathy were in the kitchen when they both heard a very loud thud, almost as though a heavy book or box had been dropped, seemingly in the room directly over the kitchen. An immediate search revealed nothing out of place.

During September 1948 a very loud crash, as of breaking crockery, was heard from the direction of the kitchen. James and Cathy rushed into the kitchen from the dining-room, to find to their astonishment, that nothing had in fact been disturbed and there was no evident reason for the loud crash they had heard. So loud was this noise that two workmen, busy mixing cement in the cottage yard, came to the door to enquire what had happened. It is interesting to recall that the loud sound of crashing crockery had been heard before at Borley, and not only by the Turners, both in the Rectory cottage, by the Coopers in 1919, and in the Rectory itself by among others Mr Mark Kerr-Pearse, one of our proconsuls at Geneva, and Mr Herbert Mayes, chauffeur to the Rev. A.C. Henning. A few weeks later a loud report, just like a pistol shot, was heard by James and Cathy Turner while they were in the kitchen. The odd thing about this incident was the loudness of the noise and the fact that it seemed to both of them immediately that it had been produced actually within the room where they were at the time.

During the summer of 1949 an apparently spectral cat made its appearance. On 28th August it was seen by both James and Cathy chasing Fred, one of their own cats. Thin and miserable in appearance, grey-white in colour, with a scraggy tail, it was quite unlike any cat in the neighbourhood. They watched as it followed Fred when he sought shelter underneath the Turner's car. Fred emerged from the other side and shot up the walnut tree for safety, but of his pursuer there was no sign! A careful search in and beneath the car, which stood on the open piece of ground at the back of the cottage, revealed no sign of any cat. It seemed certain that the mysterious furry form could not have run off across the open in another direction without being noticed by the Turners.

The same mysterious 'cat' was seen on another occasion not far from the same spot. Again it disappeared in inexplicable circumstances. Around the same time a screeching sound, such as that uttered by a cat in pain, was heard one night which did not emanate from either of the Turner's cats. It has been established that the Rev. Harry Bull was always very fond of cats (I have an original print of his favourite) and he was known to have kept anything up to thirty-four cats at one time; a fact that could well have accounted for the necessity of a Cats' Cemetery in the south-east end of the old Rectory grounds. James and Cathy Turner always looked upon their pet cats, Holly and Fred, as a protection against evil spirits.

During the course of a visit to Borley on 4th and 5th March 1950, in the company of Laurence C. Gafford of Stevenage, we conducted a number of experiments, preserved photographically, that convinced us beyond any shadow of a doubt that there were tunnels beneath the road between the church and Rectory site. It will be recalled that seven-and-a-half years later, in September 1957, contractors to the local rural council, digging a trench to lay water mains, cut through brickwork and came upon the tunnel, in excellent condition, which was immediately explored and photographed by my friend for many years, Len Sewell, who for a time lived in a caravan on the Rectory site and kept me informed of local activities. In his will he left me all his Borley photographs and collections of cuttings and correspondence. Of perhaps more interest from a personal point of view was the experience that befell Laurence Gafford and I during that night in March 1950 which we spent partly in the Turners' lounge which they kindly put at our disposal. This room was situated immediately beneath the Turners' bedroom and had a doorway that led directly onto the old Rectory grounds. Electrical and other controls were placed in and around the church and Rectory site and we began our vigil at 1 a.m. after James and Cathy had retired to bed. After checking all our controls we returned to the lounge, sitting by the fire intermittently until 3.15 a.m. when we both heard heavy footsteps and muffled voices from overhead. Laurence Gafford commented that the Turners were having a disturbed night. After a further check on our controls we returned to the lounge when we were both surprised to again hear heavy footfalls and muttering and the same sounds were heard yet again under similar circumstances at 4.15 a.m. On each occasion the sounds ceased a few seconds after we first became conscious of them. The sounds lasted perhaps a total of twenty seconds on each occasion.

When the Turners appeared for breakfast we told them of the sounds we had heard but they assured us they had both slept soundly and had not awakened until just before they arose. On being told that we had three times heard movement, footsteps and the sound of muffled conversation from the direction of their room during the night, they were not surprised and pointed out that on occasions the Coopers had heard whispering in the indicated corner of that room. The Rev. John C. Dening was also spending the night at the cottage on that occasion but he was sleeping in a front bedroom on the first floor overlooking the church. He had been up late the previous evening and slept soundly throughout the night and heard nothing untoward. On this visit James Turner kindly presented me with a relic from the old Rectory, a boundary stone carved with the initials 'H.B.' – the Rev. Henry Bull who built Borley Rectory in 1863. It now graces my garden.

In August 1950 a new discovery was made at Borley. The find is best described in a letter James Turner sent me dated 24th August 1950:

> . . . This morning while walking from the cottage at Borley into the garden, passing the dahlia bed and along the path across the old Bull orchard which is bounded on one side by the brick wall of the stables, I noticed for the first time a break in the brickwork. It looked as if someone in the past had cut a hole there and filled it with cement. On going closer (to see why anyone would want to make a hole at eye level) I discovered that what I had taken for cement was, in fact, a carved stone face built into the wall at the time of building the shed. The face is clearly defined though very old. The odd thing, to me, is that for three years or more I have been up and down the path and never noticed it. I am going to dig beneath it to see if it marks the spot of anything. It is a double brick wall and I hope to remove a brick on the other side and see if there is anything behind it. [This was done but nothing unusual was found.]

Not unnaturally I was very interested. Many times on my visits to Borley, and especially on the first occasion in May 1947 when, in the company of Tom Brown, I spent most of the night only a few yards from the spot, I must have passed close to the Face-in-the-Wall. There had been an appreciable amount of ivy covering parts of the wall and the luxuriant growth of this evergreen probably hid for many years this curiosity.

On 10th September 1950 James Turner wrote to let me know that 'digging has revealed what looks like earlier foundations, but it is a little early to be sure. What looks like a flint wall has come to light.' He enclosed a sketch of the Face executed by Ronald Blythe, then working at Colchester Library but later to become a much respected writer on East Anglian rural life. On 24th September 1950 (it took the Turners over a year to find a buyer), accompanied by the Rev. John C Dening, Tommy Frankland and Peter Heywood of Ewell, I visited Borley again and was able to examine the Face in situ and I met and congratulated Ronnie Blythe on his excellent drawing. The Face appeared to me to be medieval and it measured seven-and-a-half inches across its widest part and five-and-a-half inches in height. It was built into the wall at a height of six feet from ground level. As I have already stated when visiting the Bulls at Chilton Lodge on 8th July 1951 Ethel Bull told me she remembered the Face and she thought it had been found lying about somewhere and when the wall was built, probably at the suggestion of one of the children, it was built into the wall by, she thought, her brother Harry. It occurred to me therefore that it could well be a remnant of a building that previously occupied the Rectory site.

Although the Turners were, perhaps understandably, always reluctant to discuss such matters, in view of the publicity given to anything pertaining to the Borley haunting and James's religious scruples, both James and Cathy told me in confidence, that they had both contacted an entity claiming to be the Rev. Harry Bull (as had two of Harry's sisters, Harry Price, the Rev. Guy Eric Smith and his wife, Miss Lucie Kaye and Mr V.C. Wall in June 1929 – Ethel Bull told me incidentally that she was utterly convinced that no living person could have known the answers given to her questions that night – no one but her dead brother) and furthermore both James and Cathy were convinced that they had glimpsed a nun-like figure near the Nun's Walk one summer evening and seen a tall male clerical figure in the churchyard that disappeared in mysterious circumstances. Since both James and Cathy have been dead now for a good many years, I feel sure they would release me from my promise. They told me they had related these experiences to Harry Price, also under the promise of confidentiality, and I have a letter from Harry Price to James Turner saying that he had 'accumulated a lot more evidence for the haunting of the Rectory' and adding, 'I should much like to include your own experiences in Borley III'. Alas it was not to be but for the sake of completeness the Turners' experiences are now published.

* * * * * *

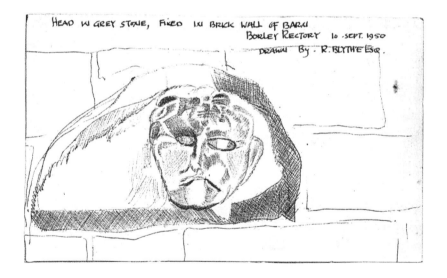

HEAD IN GREY STONE, FIXED IN BRICK WALL OF BARN
BORLEY RECTORY 10 ·SEPT. 1950
DRAWN BY · R·BLYTHE Esq.

Alfred and Ethel Bull and the present author at Chilton Lodge

James and Catherine Turner standing on what was left of the Nun's Walk in 1947

PART 9

Visits to Chilton Lodge

Visits to Chilton Lodge

[Chilton Lodge, Cornard Road, Sudbury was a solid Georgian building which the Bull family purchased in 1920 when most of the surviving children of the Rev. H.D.E. Bull moved there, leaving the Rev. Harry Bull, his wife Ivy and her daughter Constance to inhabit Borley Rectory.]

Ethel, Constance and Alfred Bull were three of the surviving Bull children who latterly lived at Chilton Lodge where I visited them on several occasions, the first in 1951 when Ethel seemed to be in charge as she was on my subsequent visits. I visited Chilton Lodge by myself, with my wife, Dr Peter Hilton-Rowe, the Rev. John C. Dening and others. My wife got on famously with the Bulls and when Ethel discovered that Joyce was interested in blue and white china, she gave her a beautiful miniature blue and white plate that once graced Borley Rectory. I visited Chilton Lodge with my good friend Peter Hilton-Rowe, a former Bank of England official, who took photographs at Borley for Harry Price and once caught a glimpse of the famous ghost nun at the same gate where the Bull sisters saw the nun in 1900. In the company of John Dening, with whom I explored the hauntings at Borley and Langenhoe, I remember enjoying a splendid meal with the Bulls. Later, as the Rev. John Dening, he served parishes at Warrington, Bournemouth and Yeovil and wrote books about the haunted church at Langenhoe. I was fortunate enough to meet other members of the Bull family there and elsewhere. All of them had vivid memories of 'the most haunted house in England' and of their brother Harry and of the Borley ghosts. Chilton Lodge was full of heavy furniture and pictures and it seemed to me that the transferred Bulls did their best to make the place as much like their former, haunted, home as possible.

I always remember what were almost the first words that Ethel Bull said to me on my first visit when I asked about the Borley ghost nun: 'oh yes, I saw the nun on at least two occasions.' She spoke in matter of fact tones and as an unemotional statement of fact.

There was of course the famous 28th July 1900 sighting when Ethel, Freda and Mabel were returning to their home from a garden party. It was still quite light as they entered the drive gate and started towards the house, then, at the same time they said, they all saw the figure of a nun dressed in black with bowed head, her hands clasped as though in prayer. She was walking or gliding along the path on the other side of the lawn, a path that became known as the Nun's Walk. I found it an unforgettable experience to hear an account of this famous episode first hand and I asked Ethel if she could remember her feelings at the time – all these years later. She replied at once, 'Certainly, I was scared stiff!'

One of the sisters ran ahead of the others and fetched an older sister, Elsie (christened Caroline and also known as Dodie). She came out of the Rectory, immediately saw the figure herself and went towards her, thinking it was a nun on some errand of mercy who had become confused or lost but when she was within a couple of yards of the figure, it completely vanished. If this account is accepted we are faced with a figure seen by three people simultaneously, then by another from a different direction, all in daylight by responsible young women (daughters of a clergyman) who all told the same story of the incident for the rest of their lives. Less than four months later Ethel saw the ghost nun again, this time in the company of the Rectory cook, apparently leaning over a gate and, interestingly enough, a cousin, staying at the house at the time, also saw the same figure in the same place.

Ethel told me that she 'quite expected' and had little doubt that their parents knew all about the ghost 'but we were never told'. That is why some of the family, Walter and Gerald in particular, were somewhat sceptical of the ghost story since such things were never discussed within the family and these two brothers were not at home all that often. Walter, I learned, spent much of his life at sea and was only very rarely at Borley Rectory. I recall asking Ethel about the seance in the Blue Room on 13th June 1929 attended by Harry Price, Lucie Kaye, V.C. Wall, Guy and Mabel Smith and Ethel and her sister Mabel. Price states: 'About two o'clock in the morning we were all startled by the new cake of soap jumping out of its dish, striking the edge of the water ewer and bouncing on the floor. The washstand was at the far end of the room; no one was near it, as we were seated round the mirror . . . Everyone saw the phenomenon'. ('Most Haunted House in England' p. 43). The journalist Wall's report of the event read: 'Finally came the most astonishing event of the night. A cake of soap on the washstand was lifted and thrown heavily on to a china jug standing on the floor with such force that the soap was deeply marked. All of us were at the other side of the room when this happened'. But Ethel told me, 'We were none of us in the room when the piece of soap jumped out of its washstand' and she repeated this in a letter to me dated 22nd September 1954. To me her insistence that the 'jumping soap' was not actually witnessed by anyone makes her story of the famous 28th July sighting of the nun all the more convincing; having known Ethel I do feel that if there had been any confusion or possibility of malobservation, she would have said so. In the event she and her sisters (Mabel died in 1936) hardly altered their story in the slightest concerning this strange and undoubtedly memorable event.

I asked Ethel Bull about Mrs Mabel Smith's letter to the "Church Times" in October 1945 when she said: '. . . I would like to state definitely that neither my husband nor myself believed the house [Borley Rectory] haunted by anything else but rats and local superstition. We left the Rectory because of its broken-down condition, but certainly found nothing to fear there.' Having met and talked with Mrs Smith I said that I wondered how Ethel Bull felt about that statement. She replied, 'All nonsense, she used to shriek with fright' and she put this in writing to me in a letter dated 22nd September 1954.

The surviving members of the Bull family always welcomed my wife and I and anyone we cared to bring with us to Chilton Lodge, ('that old-world house' as Harry Price called it) as long as they were alive and it really did seem like stepping back into the Victorian era to take tea there: the great table, covered by a spotless white linen tablecloth; the delicate floral and fluted china and the silver tea service with its enormous sugar bowl. The leisured meal in summer invariably included a great pile of home-grown strawberries, a glass jug of fresh cream and a glass bowl of caster sugar, home-made fruit cake and cucumber and cress sandwiches. The heavy furniture, leather-seated armchairs and thick furnishings all added to the sombre atmosphere but I found the hospitable Bulls were friendly, open and always ready to discuss anything and answer any questions. Looking down on us from the wall were portraits of their father, the Rev. H.D.E. Bull with his mutton-chop whiskers, and their brother, Harry who enjoyed boxing as a young man but disappointed his family by marrying a Roman Catholic nurse with a daughter and who had a lifelong habit of falling asleep at any time of the day and wherever he might be; yet he was described to me by a doctor who knew him well when he was at university as 'one of the most normal men you could meet'. Be that as it may he undoubtedly claimed to see and hear the ghost nun on many occasions and to have seen and heard the phantom coach and horses and to have experienced a wealth of seemingly inexplicable happenings.

Each time I visited Chilton Lodge – perhaps nine or ten times – I always thought of the various people who had visited Chilton Lodge before me and those who were to come after.

Harry Bull and his wife Ivy and a young Constance Brackenby had visited. When I asked about that visit, Ethel said, perhaps enlighteningly, 'Well, of course Harry was always welcome and he came when he could . . .' She said Harry Bull was very popular in the village and always found time to chat about boxing, cats or the Borley ghosts that he never tired of discussing. He always wanted to talk to the ghost but never succeeded in carrying on a conversation with the phantom form he said he saw on numerous occasions.

The Bulls' cousin Lionel Foyster had been to Chilton Lodge with his brother Arthur – and the enigmatic Marianne. The Bull sisters I spoke to felt Marianne was probably mediumistic because psychic phenomena seemed to occur wherever she happened to be; they didn't like her and Ethel once described her to Sidney Glanville (when he visited Chilton Lodge) as 'mad as a hatter' and Constance called her 'a little beast'. When I taxed Ethel on this matter, she said, 'Did I really say that? Well she was very self-centred you know, and eccentric and she did some very disreputable things. She wasn't a happy woman, we felt . . .' I met Arthur Foyster several times at his home in Pinner and knew Sidney Glanville and his family; we met at different times in Paul Tabori's flat in Kensington, at the Strand Palace Hotel, and at the charming Glanville home in Fittleworth.

Guy Eric Smith visited Chilton Lodge when he was the newly inducted Rector of Borley accompanied by his 'somewhat nervous' wife Mabel in 1929. Later visits followed and Ethel found him 'quite charming but an ignoramus in psychic matters'. His wife she never liked; 'she seemed frightened of shadows' and told them she 'had some silly idea about writing a best-selling book'.

Harry Price and his then secretary Lucie Kaye visited Chilton Lodge on the occasion of his first visit to Borley in June 1929. He found the Bull sisters, Ethel, Freda and Constance (at that time) 'very charming and cultured, and quite ready to give any information in their possession concerning Borley Rectory; and willing to relate their personal experiences of the nun and other phenomena'. Harry Price again visited Chilton Lodge in March 1939, this time in the company of Sidney Glanville.

Lord Charles Hope visited the Bulls at Chilton Lodge in July 1929. I had a long talk with Eton educated Lord Charles, the second son of the First Marquess of Linlithgow, at an S.P.R. lecture meeting in 1956. On the Bulls I remember he said, 'Well, whatever criticisms are levelled at the Bull sisters, they can never be accused of changing their story!' Sadly I have to say this was said as though it was a criticism. Hope was a close associate of Harry Price in his Rudi Schneider experiments and they visited Borley together but after Hope privately arranged to test the medium himself, without telling Price who had organised everything involving Rudi over a ten year period, including more than 2000 letters (still in the Harry Price Library), Price showed his displeasure in no uncertain terms and things were never satisfactorily healed between them.

Ethel Bull told me she remembered W.H. Salter from the S.P.R. visiting Chilton Lodge in October 1931. He had been to Borley Rectory in an attempt to persuade the Rev. Lionel Foyster to sever links with Harry Price and allow the S.P.R. to investigate the alleged haunting. Ethel remembered him saying that Price was not the ideal person to carry out confidential investigations and he said he had been to see Lionel Foyster and thought he had convinced him not to have anything more to do with Price – could he rely on her and her sisters to do likewise? Ethel said she had made no comment but thought he had a cheek to ask and later Lionel told her he had no intention of taking any notice of what Salter had said. I recall once having lunch with Salter and Mollie Goldney, at that time two of the most powerful people at the S.P.R. They paid for the lunch at a restaurant near Tavistock Square where the S.P.R. headquarters was then situated. When I defended Price after Salter made a completely unjustified and derogatory remark about him, Mollie jumped in saying 'Oh, I hope you are not a Price worshipper?' A typical nasty and cutting remark that she was capable of making at a moment's notice. At other times she could be the most charming of people and I have happy memories of visiting her at her enormous flat and enjoying her company at Ghost Club Society gatherings. I always remember her making a little speech at one of our Annual Dinners and saying: 'I was beginning to feel that this Club would never be what it was in Harry Price's day but now that Peter Underwood has taken us under his wing and arranged such magnificent visits to haunted houses, I have revised my opinion. It is something Harry would have approved of and I know he would have been very proud of the Club as it is today'. Salter and Goldney visited Chilton Lodge in August 1950 accompanied by the Rev. S. Austin (a Borley sceptic).

In March 1938 Flight-Lieutenant Carter Jonas (later Air Commodore) and his friend Flight-Lieutenant Caunter visited the Bulls at Chilton Lodge while spending a couple of nights at Borley Rectory. Although they had experienced apparent phenomena on previous visits (they were two of Price's official investigators) this time they were unlucky and found 'the house and grounds at night were as still as a vault'. My wife and I became long-time friends with Jonas and his wife Gina and we often visited them at their beautiful home in Fowey. When they left Cornwall Jonas presented me with his files on hauntings and his personal records, Borley log book and correspondence with Harry Price.

Sir George and Lady Whitehouse and their nephew Richard Whitehouse had often been guests at Chilton Lodge. Ethel told me she found Lady Whitehouse a charming and kind person who readily accepted that Borley Rectory was haunted. She and young Richard seemed quite fond of Marianne Foyster, speaking warmly of her and her love for the children. Richard Whitehouse she thought pleasant enough but found his complete trust of and infatuation with Marianne hard to accept. I had copious correspondence with Dom Richard Whitehouse OSB, as he became, in the late 1950s and spent hours talking to him about Borley in general and Marianne in particular at my London club in 1956. The gist of our conversation was confirmed by him in writing at my request on 6th August 1956 and forms Appendix C in Robert

Hastings' 'Examination of the SPR Borley Report' in the Proceedings of that Society, Part 201 Volume 55 dated March 1969.

Bob Hastings too visited Chilton Lodge and talked with the surviving Bull sisters and brother. I came to know Bob well when he was compiling and writing his critique of the SPR allegations and at his home in Wales, at my home in Hampshire, at my London club and at a room at the SPR we often 'tired the sun with talking and sent him down the sky'.

Seymour J. de Lotbiniere OBE, a much respected BBC employee visited Chilton Lodge when he was producing a broadcast about the Borley haunting. He first joined the BBC in 1932 and became in turn Director of Outside Broadcasts, Head of Television Outside Broadcasts and Assistant Controller of all Television Programmes. He was one of Price's investigators and he bore witness to new wall writings appearing under test conditions. Years later he produced a television film about the Dracula story, in which I took part, and on location in Essex we talked about Borley and its mysteries. He was still convinced, some thirty-five years after the event, that the wall markings he witnessed in July 1937 could not have been executed by human hands.

Yet another visitor to Chilton Lodge who was deeply interested in the Borley ghosts was Brigadier C.A.L Brownslow DSO who called there, on invitation, in February 1954. He had visited Borley for the first time the previous year, meeting the Bacon and Williams families who then resided at Priory Cottage (as it was then called) and hearing about the sightings of the ghost nun, the mysterious fires, the strange shadowy figures, the unaccountable smells and the inevitable and inexplicable footsteps; all experienced by the occupants he talked to. At Chilton Lodge Ethel showed him half-a-dozen large original photographs of the house and garden of Borley Rectory (she subsequently gave these photographs to me) and he was fascinated to recognize many of the pictures, the china, glass and furniture in the photographs that had been moved from Borley Rectory to Chilton Lodge and were now in the rooms he visited. Ethel talked to him, as she talked to me on other occasions, of the Bull family at Borley Rectory being a normal and happy family and she retained a wealth of delightful memories of her days at the Rectory. I talked with the Brigadier at his home in Sudbury and corresponded with him both before and after his visits. There is no doubt that he was completely convinced of the authenticity of the Borley haunting.

In a letter dated 17th August 1952 Miss Ethel Bull informed me that the Rev. A.C. Henning (then Rector of Borley-cum-Liston) and Mrs Henning had been to see them. I came to know the Hennings quite well over some ten years and I frequently visited Liston Rectory where they lived and heard all about the many strange experiences he and his family had endured – including phantom organ music and movement of objects inside the church – first hand. Many of these happenings Henning published in his book "Haunted Borley" 1949 (I possess a copy personally inscribed to me) which was typed for him by James Turner, at that time resident at the Rectory Cottage, on consideration that Henning did not publish any reported happenings involving the Turners and did not publish their names.

In April 1953 Dr Eric John Dingwall and Trevor Hall and his family visited Chilton Lodge and he wrote of the visit as 'an enjoyable and interesting occasion being entertained to tea by Ethel and Alfred Bull'. Dingwall I had long known through his association with the British Museum Reading Room, where he was an official and I was a frequent visitor and of course our joint association with the Society for Psychical Research; while I possess reams of correspondence with Trevor Hall, although I never had the doubtful pleasure of actually meeting that particular 'gentleman'. He always seems to me to fit a quotation from Sir Arthur Conan Doyle's "A Study in Scarlet": 'His ignorance was as remarkable as his knowledge'.

James and Catherine Turner visited the Bulls (what a pity Ethel did not keep a Visitors' Book!) and were treated to firsthand accounts of paranormal happenings, including the famous 1900 sighting. My wife and I came to know the Turners well and we liked them both enormously. We visited them at their successive homes: The Mill House, Belchamp Walter (of which I possess a charming oil painting) and Hilltop, Grundisburgh near Woodbridge in Suffolk and eventually Cornwall. We visited and stayed with them at Primrose Cottage, just inland from Treyarnon Bay (purchased from the Turners by renowned actor Joss Ackland), Trenague just outside Wadebridge and the cottage at St Teath where sadly James died very suddenly. Subsequently we used to stay regularly with Cathy at her delightful flat at St Giles House above Wadebridge. Both James and Cathy visited us at our homes in Twickenham and in Hampshire. They both found the Borley haunting somewhat overwhelming, especially when they lived at the old Rectory cottage, but they came to accept that much of the reported phenomena were factual although they sometimes seemed somewhat sceptical of the Bull sisters famous sighting of the ghost nun in 1900, thinking that perhaps the story had become engraved on their memories to such an extent that it was impossible to say any longer whether the story was factual or not, but, as James used to say, 'forget the Bulls, the evidence for paranormal activity at Borley is established by a wealth of other evidence'.

The visitors to Chilton Lodge over the years reads like a Who's Who of everyone who had anything to do with the Borley story and those I have mentioned were just a few who entered the portals of that hospitable homestead. In 2001 Mrs S.M. Brotherwood, Town Clerk of Sudbury, informed me that Chilton Lodge was 'bulldozed' in the late 1960s and new properties were constructed by a local builder.

* * * * * *

PART 10

John L. Randall on Harry Price and Borley

John L. Randall on Harry Price and Borley

[John L. Randall took a four-year in-depth look at the life and work of Harry Price; he has written the entry on the best-known British psychical researcher of the twentieth century for the "New Dictionary of National Biography" and he has addressed the S.P.R. on the subject. The July 2000 issue of the Journal of The Society for Psychical Research contained an 18-page article by him on "Harry Price: The Case for the Defence". These are his comments about the Borley haunting.]

. . . I have come across numerous books and articles which cite the famous 'debunking' report on Borley Rectory (Dingwall, Goldney and Hall, 1956) but very few mention the criticisms of that report by Michael Coleman (The Borley Report: some criticisms, SPR Journal 38, 1956) and Robert Hastings (An Examination of the 'Borley Report' SPR Proceedings 55, 1969) . . .

There is direct evidence of at least two 'dirty tricks' played upon Price by members of the SPR. On October 9th, 1931, W.H. Salter travelled to Borley to try to persuade the Rector, the Revd Lionel Foyster, to sever his links with Price and accept the ministrations of the SPR instead (Banks, "The Enigma of Borley Rectory", 1996). Since Price had been studying the phenomena at the allegedly haunted rectory since June 1929, this was a clear example of unprofessional conduct. The reader may like to imagine how the BMA would respond to a medical practitioner who tried to steal a colleague's patients. Yet this highly unethical act is not mentioned by Gregory in her article on "Ethics and Psychical Research" in which Price is condemned unreservedly (Gregory, SPR Journal 47, 1974). It has been claimed, by Salter's defenders, that he acted ethically in that he was trying to prevent undue publicity at Borley. However, he had no right to interfere at all – the SPR is not a psychic police force. As for publicity, this had already happened, via the "Daily Mirror" (10th June 1929), before Price went near the place. The second 'dirty trick' had more serious repercussions . . . [It concerned Lord Charles Hope and the Rudi Schneider experiments, not the Borley haunting.]

Harry Price died on Easter Monday, 29th March 1948; he was 67 years old. Within a few months of his death the attacks on his reputation began. Charles Sutton, a journalist who had been present at some of the Schneider experiments, wrote in a popular magazine that he had caught Price faking phenomena at Borley (Sutton, The Meditations of Charles Sutton, "Inky Way Annual, Book 2" 1948). W.H. Salter pressed his SPR colleagues to launch a re-investigation of the case. The result was the publication, in 1956, of the now famous 'Borley Report' (Dingwall, Goldney and Hall, 1956). The 180-page report was essentially a systematic attack on the honesty and integrity of Harry Price; it was, as Renee Haynes put it, "the case for the prosecution". Every event was interpreted in such a way as to present Price in the worst possible light, and alternative interpretations were played down or ignored.

The Sutton allegations and the Borley Report (which drew heavily upon them) came as severe shocks to Price's widow and to his many friends. The general feeling was one of indignation and dismay. Mrs Lucie Meeker (nee Kay) who had been Price's secretary, denied that there had been any such incident as that described by Sutton and added:-

> . . . it is my considered conviction that Harry Price never, at any time, faked phenomena. I worked with him in close collaboration for some five years and, indeed, remained friends with him to the day of his death, and I am convinced he was a man of unimpeachable integrity. (Hastings)

That seems to have been the verdict of nearly all the people who worked at all closely with Price. Sydney Glanville, his chief collaborator at Borley, described him as "an astonishing worker" for psychical research and a friend for whom he had "a very great regard and respect" (Tabori, "Harry Price: The Biography of a Ghost-Hunter", 1974). Geoffrey H. Motion, a neighbour of Price's who also accompanied him to Borley, was also convinced that he did not fake phenomena. (This information was the result of a personal communication from Mr Motion's son, Mr Barry Motion.) The Revd George Royle (the Rector always disclaimed any knowledge of Price's psychical activities; however, he accompanied him on at least one poltergeist investigation, as is shown by the article and photographs in "Picture Post", 22nd December 1945) Rector of Pulborough from 1944 to 1970, said that he counted Price among his best and most loyal friends, and told enquirers that he regarded him as "a man of complete integrity" (Royle in an address at Pulborough, 1948, preserved at County Record Office Chichester; Underwood, "The Ghost Hunters: Who They are and What They Do" 1985). The Bishop of Chichester, Dr George Bell, described him as "not only a famous and highly honoured worker in the field of Psychical Research, but a devoted member of the Church of England" (Bell in an address at Pulborough, 1948, preserved at County Record Office, Chichester). Price had been made a churchwarden of St Mary's, Pulborough, just a few weeks before his death.

It is clear, then, that during Price's lifetime most of his associates, including several eminent churchmen, regarded him as a man of honour and trustworthiness. Yet if the authors of the Borley Report were correct, he had perpetrated one of the most impudent frauds in the whole history of psychical research. But some members of the SPR felt uneasy at the obviously biased nature of the Report, and in 1965 a grant of £50 was given to Robert J. Hastings towards the expenses involved in a re-examination of the case. The resulting 'Hastings Report' was published in 1969; it uncovered a number of errors in the original evidence, and was widely interpreted by the media as the official exoneration of Harry Price. To correct this impression the Honorary Secretary of the Society, John Cutten, wrote to "New Scientist" magazine, pointing out that the Society holds no corporate views:–

> The Society has never attacked Mr Price, nor is it about to exonerate him, as the statement to which you refer claimed. We may publish papers in our Journal or Proceedings, and at a later date publish opposing views of other members; but providing facilities for free expression in our publications does not imply that the Society identifies itself with any particular opinion. (Cutten, Letter to the Editor, "New Scientist" 3rd April, 1969).

This is technically correct, of course, but it is surely also rather naïve. When, as happened in 1956, a learned society publishes a book-length attack on a man's reputation, it is bound to be seen by the general public as representing the views of that society. The Borley Report was badly flawed and very heavily biased, and Hastings believed that the Society should not have published it. He felt that the attack on Price may have opened the door to a subsequent wave of denigration of other psychical researchers (Hastings, 1969).

Trevor Henry Hall was an estate agent, local magistrate, amateur conjurer and writer of popular books on Sherlock Holmes and Dorothy L. Sayers. In 1954 he was awarded the Perrott Studentship in Psychical Research, although he was not then a member of the SPR (he joined, but only for a short time, a few years later). He was said to be doing research into "special conditions which appear favourable to the emergence of ESP", but I have found no evidence that it was ever published. Although Hall never met or corresponded with Harry Price, he seems to have conceived an almost fanatical hatred for the famous ghost-hunter. Hall joined the team working on the Borley Report and, according to his own account (Hall, "New Light on Old Ghosts" 1965) was responsible for four of the eight chapters it contained. Ivan Banks has surmised, I think correctly, that it was the participation of Trevor Hall which gave rise to the uncompromisingly hostile tone of the Borley Report (Banks, ibid 1996).

Robert Hastings makes the important point that Price's work should be judged by his research files, not by his popular writing. Popular accounts inevitably over-simplify, and therefore to some extent falsify. In the case of Borley, the sheer quantity and complexity of the material makes it unreasonable to expect that a popular account could be written without any errors at all. In general, Price seems to have been far more meticulous in his checking and referencing of factual material than many modern writers; but like all of us, he made mistakes.

To the general public, Price's name is inextricably coupled to that of Borley Rectory. This is a pity since some of his best work was done in the early years, before he had even heard of Borley. Even so, the Borley case remains the most fully documented example of a haunting in the annals of psychical research and Price's accumulation of a vast dossier of eye-witness reports is a major contribution to the study of spontaneous phenomena.

* * * * * *

A signed photograph of Harry Price
that is in the possession of the present author.

PART 11

Welcome to Harry Price's Home

Harry Price Library.

Welcome to Harry Price's Home

[In 1967 I visited Harry Price's home on the banks of the River Arun at Pulborough in Sussex, at the kind invitation of his widow Constance Mary Price, the only daughter of Robert Hastings Knight. At the time of Price's sudden death in 1948 he and Constance had been happily married for almost forty years and nearly twenty years after his death it was almost as though he had just popped out for a moment.]

On Sunday 20th October 1968, in the company of my friend and fellow Borley student and Ghost Club Society Life Member Steuart Kiernander I called at Arun Bank, Pulborough, Sussex at eleven o'clock in the morning as arranged with Mrs Constance Price, widow of Harry Price who had died on 28th March 1948.

As we approached the porch of the house along the shrub-lined stone path I caught a glimpse of a grey-haired lady looking out of the window of the front door and my knock was acknowledged by the quick bark of a Scottie dog. After a moment the door was cautiously opened by a rather dumpy, tinted-spectacled figure, about five feet and six inches in height with a healthy glow to her cheeks. She acknowledged that she was Mrs Constance Price and in return ascertained that I was Peter Underwood, a friend of Dr Paul Tabori and Sidney Glanville and that I knew and enjoyed her late husband's books. I wondered whether she would very much mind if I photographed the Borley Bell that hung over her husband's workshop. Constance Price was deaf and asked me my name again and then graciously agreed to my request and directed me round the house, saying she would meet me there. Suddenly she asked me where my camera was and I said I had left it in my car and would she mind very much if my friend, who was with me, joined me. She readily agreed and while she disappeared into the house I returned to the car.

Steuart and I made our way round the side of the house, through a green gate and emerged at the side of the garage that must have once housed Price's beloved Rolls Royce and there was Mrs Price, with her Scottie (now quiet and friendly) just at the foot of high

148

steps that led to the balcony at the back of the house. It was from this balcony that Richard S. Lambert, for ten years Editor of "The Listener", took the celebrated photograph he used in his volume, "Ariel and All his Quality" (1940).

Mrs Price showed us the bell, larger than I had imagined and heavier, hanging over the closed green doors marked 'Workshop'. Mrs Price said she used the bell occasionally to summon her brother and sister-in-law who lived next door. She said she and Harry had been school pupils together at New Cross, they had been sweethearts all their lives and when they had married, at Pulborough Church, just over the road, they had lived next door for a year before having Arun Bank built and moving there in 1907. (She *did* say 1907, although in his autobiography Harry Price says he married in 1908 so presumably she meant to say 1909).

I asked Mrs Price whether she would have a photograph taken with me and she at first declined but I prevailed on her and she agreed. She and I moved over and stood beneath the Borley Bell (which I rang – for the first time) and Steuart took a photograph. Mrs Price was shading her eyes from the sun (it was a brilliant day although October) and so I suggested she stood on the other side of me and looked at me rather than into the sun. Steuart then took another photograph [which is reproduced in this volume] and then he and I took several photographs of the bell.

We chatted for a while, admiring the splendid view from the balcony, and when I turned the conversation to Harry Price's death, saying it came as a shock to everyone who knew his work; she said it was completely unexpected for although he had spoken of occasionally feeling pain over his heart, they had not thought it anything serious and he had not even consulted a doctor. She added that it was sad because he had just written the first chapter for a third book on haunted Borley Rectory and drafted out what the book would contain but she did not know what would now happen since she had no interest in psychic research and there did not appear to be anyone to carry on his work. She went on to say that she was 87, just the previous week; and although she lived alone she had lots of relatives around. As we prepared to say 'Goodbye' Mrs Price asked us whether we would like a glass of sherry before we left.

We accepted and she asked us to wait on the white painted balcony while she fetched some glasses. She went inside the house but re-appeared a moment later with a bamboo table followed by a bottle of exquisite sherry, two sherry glasses and some plain biscuits – on a silver tray. She asked us to help ourselves, saying she would not have a glass at the moment.

We looked out over the garden with its octagonal pond which Mrs Price told us Harry used to keep stocked with golden carp which he was fond of. She thought she had lost them all one winter when the pond was frozen over for weeks but afterwards, once the thaw had set in, they came up, very tame, and looking for food. Next day a heron had the lot! Herons came up the Arun (which flowed along the bottom of the garden) and her sister often had a kingfisher in her garden. Mrs Price told us she had had a nervous breakdown the previous year, brought on, she thought, by overwork . . . It was a lovely and tranquil spot: away in the distance we could see the rolling Sussex downs – without a human habitation in sight.

Then, as we again prepared to leave, Mrs Price said, 'You may as well come through this way' and she led us into the house. We found ourselves in a hall which ran the length of the house and she showed us into the room on our left where I spotted the original portrait in oils of Harry Price by John Dumayne, painted in 1900 and reproduced in "Search for Truth". There were several examples of Price's photographic art, framed and hanging on the walls including one of Pulborough Church and another of a favourite dog they used to own. There were other prints and pictures and the room, typically Victorian with its heavy furniture, still had a peaceful and quiet feeling about it. I asked whether this was the room where Harry had died and Mrs Price said 'no' and led us to the front room, next door to where we were, at the front of the house, again on our left as we walked towards the front door. She showed us into the Study; saying this was where Harry had died. He had returned home after posting a letter and had sat down in his favourite chair on the left of the fireplace. She invited me to sit in it myself if I wished to and I did. She said when he came in that afternoon she had said she would make them both a cup of tea and when she returned with it, he was dead in the chair. A great shock for her but she said he must have had some heart trouble and sometimes he used to say his heart was pounding. He had not been well the whole of his last week. After he died Mrs Price said she was inundated with letters, literally hundreds of them, many asking about the Ghost Club. She was interested to hear that I had helped to revive the Club in 1954 and that I was actively associated with The Ghost Cub Society. 'Harry had overworked himself,' she said. 'He never stopped . . . He was a clever man, really,' she added.

Talking about Borley she said she knew nothing about it but she thought Mrs Goldney was a two-faced woman and Eric Dingwall was no better. They had often been there and she had looked on them as friends.

She had not read the S.P.R. book: Mr Walker, the trustee from the Midland Bank had advised her not to and she had not done so. She said she always liked Sidney Glanville but there had been another man, long after Harry's death, [presumably Trevor Hall] 'snooping about and asking the rector and other people questions about what kind of man Harry had been . . .'

We were shown Harry Price's desk and again there were framed photographs on the wall, four of Harry Price himself including two taken in that very room. There were relics from the First World War, including parts of shells and cartridge caps, which he had made, lying on the desk and there were some geological specimens that he had collected and some that he and Constance had brought back from holidays, one in Scotland, she told us. And of course there were the books; some in glass-fronted bookcases including a complete mint-condition set of his own books, complete with jackets. Mrs Price said the University of London had been very good and could have taken immediate possession but had left them with her for her lifetime – 'I don't expect,' she added with a smile, 'that they thought it would be twenty years!' When I asked what would eventually happen to the Borley Bell, she said that rested with the executors and the University of London. [In fact soon after Mrs Price's death the University and the executors Midland Bank presented me with the massive Borley Bell which now rests in my garden.]

At length, warm with the kindness of this charming little lady we made our way to the front door, Mrs Price standing there seeing us out and waving as we made our way back to the car, parked nearby in front of high wooden gates that must have been used on innumerable occasions by Harry Price since they led to the garage. To reach the front door we had to pass a coat rack and could not help but notice hanging there several of Harry Price's coats, several of his hats, and several of his walking sticks stood in the corner. It was almost as though he had just gone out and would be back again very shortly.

* * * * * *

Mrs Constance Price, widow of Harry,
with the present author at Arun Bank, Pulborough in 1967.

PART 12

"Night at Borley Rectory"
(a poem)

"Night at Borley Rectory"

[I wrote this poem after my first visit to Borley in 1947. I tried to convey some of the phenomena experienced rather than an account of the night we spent there.]

The tall dark trees swish ominously
A branch of the elm tree creaks,
The moon lights up queer shapes on the ground,
And the hinge of the yard-gate squeaks.

The church tower gleams between the trees
'Gainst the ever-darkening sky
A weird white shape glides up the Nun's Walk
And an owl flies silently by.

Raps and taps come from the site
Where the old Rectory stood
Footsteps creep between the trees –
Eyes look out from the wood.

What drama has left its mark for ever
And drenched the very atmosphere,
Of this so quiet, tranquil spot
That night is never peaceful here?

When dusk has fallen and silently gone
Then the ground itself seems in anguish
An air of expectancy lies over all
With just a suggestion of sadness.

There's a weird and wonderful something here
That rules when darkness falls
And those with eyes can see things
That have happened between these walls.

But now the dawn is breaking
And beauty and peace reign again,
And the powers that rule in the night-time
Disappear like clouds after rain.

* * * * *

BIBLIOGRAPHY

of books devoted to the Borley Rectory haunting

Banks, Ivan *The Enigma of Borley Rectory* 1996

Dingwall, Goldney and Hall, *The Haunting of Borley Rectory* 1956

Downes, Wesley *The Ghosts of Borley* 1993

Hastings, Robert *An Examination of the 'Borley Report'* 1969

Henning, A.C. *Haunted Borley* 1949

Mayerling, Louis *We Faked the Ghosts of Borley Rectory* 2000

Price, Harry *'The Most Haunted House in England'* 1940

Price, Harry *The End of Borley Rectory* 1946

Turner, James *My Life with Borley Rectory* (fictional satire) 1950

Underwood, Peter and Tabori, Paul *The Ghosts of Borley* 1973

Wood, Robert *The Widow of Borley* 1992

INDEX